The Absence Trilogy

T0349097

THE INDIA LIST

MRINAL SEN

The Absence Trilogy

EKDIN PRATIDIN · KHARIJ · EKDIN ACHANAK

Scripts Reconstructed by
Biren Das Sharma and Somnath Zutshi

LONDON NEW YORK CALCUTTA

Seagull Books, 2025

© Seagull Books, 1999

First published in English translation by Seagull Books, 1999

ISBN 978 1 80309 509 7

British Library Cataloguing-in-Publication Data
A catalogue record for this book is available from the British Library

Typeset by Seagull Books, Calcutta, India
Printed and bound by WordsWorth India, New Delhi

Contents

Introduction

The notion of calling these three films by Mrinal Sen—not necessarily linked by any commonalities—*The Absence Trilogy* might seem somewhat fanciful. Three films on apparently disparate issues. One, *Ekdin Pratidin* (col. 1979), on the tensions within a large, lower middle-class family precipitated by their oldest daughter returning home in the early hours of the morning. Another, *Kharij* (col. 1982), on a couple with aspirations of social advancement rocked by the death of their boy servant. The third, *Ekdin Achanak* (col. 1989), about a middle-class family reminiscing about—indeed attempting to reconstruct—their traumatized past, marked by the sudden disappearance of the head of the family.

The films were made over a period of ten years between 1979 and 1989; indeed, there were other films intervening between the three: several features including *Khandhar* (*The Ruins*) and *Akaler Sandhane* (*In Search of Famine*), the occasional documentary and so on. Nor did any major commonalities of theme, as I have said, link these films.

And yet, closer examination shows that the three films in question shared several areas of concern. Of these, two are of interest, particularly in terms of the apparently arbitrary reading of these films as a trilogy. What are these links in the films? The first is that each of these films attempts to examine the effects, on a group, of one member suddenly going missing, whether temporarily or permanently. The second is that in each of these three films, we see the past haunting the present. And the conjunction of the two consists in this: it is precisely in the manifestation of the absence, that is, in the gap that has been left behind by the one who is not there, that we see the shadow of the past fall.

This interrogation of the present by the past, or perhaps the underscoring of the present by an irruption of the past in its midst, is part of Mrinal Sen's continuing concerns. As one sympathetic commentator has noted, '(t)he recognition of the stream of history flowing from the past through the present into the future permeates Sen's films'.[1] Indeed, Sen himself has said that his 'spontaneous reaction' even to sites of historical interest has been to see them not 'as museum pieces but as contemporary phenomena'.[2] All the characters in these films will have to deal with the past as it obtrudes into their present. And in the course of that experience, we get a glimpse—however tangential—of the general past, so to speak, the social past, if one may so put it. What is interesting about Sen's view of the past—personal and collective—in these three instances is that the characters generally live oblivious of it. Until that is, an incident occurs that helps the past illuminate the present. A child dies; a husband and father walks out on his family; a daughter fails to return all night. And it is through the examination of the individual past that the broader social past takes shape. And the politics of the person, the family and the social whole—examined as the repercussions from one incident—are played out. And in the process, individuals sometimes gain a deeper understanding of their personal and social selves.

In each of the films, a family group under external pressure reveals its fault lines. Nor do they cohere together at the end, at least not wholly. The precipitant is a sudden loss, temporary in *Ekdin Pratidin*, but permanent in *Kharij*, and unresolved in *Ekdin Achanak*. The resultant absence enforces a form of self-examination in each individual, which changes each one's life inexorably. But who are these people whose absence causes such turmoil, so much drama? Individuals whose presence is vital to the families, obviously; but also taken for granted. Simultaneously, these individuals represent in themselves the social situation of the family they are part of, as well as its contradictions and predicaments.

For instance, there is Palan, the boy servant in *Kharij*, whose death leads to a strange rift between the young husband and wife. Brought to the city by his poor peasant father specifically for the purpose of being a servant, he is crucial to the aspirations of the couple, despite being marginal to it in all real senses of the word. He not only serves as a marker—of the couple having a certain economic status; they can afford a person for the exclusive purpose of taking care of their child—but frees the wife for other activities.

Hired to take care of their little son Pupai—despite there not being much of an age difference between the two children—the servant boy is the mirror of his younger master. Further, if Pupai gains in Palan a companion and caretaker, it is only because their social positions are the mirror images of each other. One is moving up, the other has nowhere to go; the one from a family which can afford to buy protection; the other from one that has to put its members out on the marketplace in order to survive. Indeed, it may be fair to say that more than being merely mirror images, their circumstances are carefully juxtapositioned, one against the other's. And we see how the precarious balance of this society depends on such juxtapositioning. Mamata, Pupai's mother, remarks on this on more than one occasion. On the other hand, Palan's presence is in itself a sort of absence, both in the way he is taken for granted and in the way he himself melts into the background. And yet his death, his permanent absence from t/his 'family'—presented with an almost casual understatement in the film—manifests its presence in no uncertain terms. It rocks the family and ultimately leads to a gap between Mamata and Anjan, husband and wife. It also underscores, without recourse to any unnecessary posturing, both Pupai's good fortune and the thinness of the crust he is standing on. Having experienced the loss of Palan, we realize that his presence will now linger on, in not one but two families.

In a similar manner, Chinu, the oldest daughter in *Ekdin Pratidin*, plays the role of the binding force, the one whose presence is necessary to keep the family together. Nor is this restricted to the economic sphere alone, despite her being the sole bread-earner. She is a surrogate mother for her youngest brother, Poltu. Early in the film, we see him fretting about his sister not being back. He is already in bed, having suffered a minor head injury.

POLTU. Mejdi, when'll Didi get home?

MINU. Open your mouth.

POLTU. But I've just had one!

MINU. Just open your mouth. Wider . . . now, put the book down and close your eyes.

POLTU. Mejdi . . . ?

MINU. What is it?

POLTU. When will Didi return?

MINU. She'll return . . . she'll return.

Minu rises and walks to Jhunu, who is busy studying at her desk. She puts the magazine down, as well as the tumbler. She takes a book from the pile on the table and uses it to cover the glass.

POLTU. But when . . . ?

MINU. She won't return then. Satisfied?

Later we hear other people talking about how Poltu is much closer to his sister than his mother. She also provides a role model for her younger sister Minu, who defends her sister's achievement of a certain autonomy against all and sundry. When Mother complains that Chinu is not back even though it is long past evening, it is Minu who passes the tart comment, 'She's hardly expected to clock in every day, Ma!' It is something of Chinu's warmth and quiet strength that pervades each and every member of this family. Her strength counters her father's defeatism and even her mother's fatalism. The fact that she has a job is the obverse of her brother's unemployed status. She is the one who has the wellbeing of each of the individuals that constitute this group in mind—as we see in a flashback sequence, with the camera slowly zooming in on Chinu standing against a white background and the voices of her siblings off screen:

TOPU. Hooray! Didi's got her job. The United Commercial Bank. Basic pay, Rupees 190; Dearness Allowance, Rupees 342; House Rent, Rupees 18; City Compensatory Allowance, Rupees 30; Total, Rupees 580. Bloody hell, 580!

POLTU. What fun!

TOPU. Now, you won't forget your unemployed brother, will you?

POLTU. I want a suit.

TOPU. And a dhoti for Father.

POLTU. And a sitar for Jhunu.

CHINU: Minu, don't you want . . . ?

MINU. What would I want?

CHINU: No more taking tuition for you. You can't do the housework, study and teach others, all at the same time. From now on, you just concentrate on your studies and help with the housework.

The zoom ends in the close-up of a happy-looking Chinu, her face wreathed in smiles. Slow fade to white. In this transaction, we see virtually every one of the siblings demanding something of Chinu; but only she remembers her younger sister, the one person who neither wants anything nor has anyone making demands on her behalf.

Yet, Chinu's very location in the family is such that she is the one capable of showing up the cleavages and fault lines within this group. The very idea of a young working woman in an impoverished middle-class milieu brings in its train a veritable comet's tail of contradictions. Which is not to suggest that such women are the least bit uncommon in such surroundings. Far from it. It is the very ubiquity of the circumstance which gives it its cutting edge. For it is the possible (inexorable?) growth of personal autonomy that such things as education and a career can encourage in women that is often anathema to such a milieu. Indeed, the dependency created by Chinu's being the only breadwinner for a large family can only make her independence—it has become her's automatically—even more difficult to bear. We are reminded of this at regular intervals. A young woman out in the wide world, cut off from the protective gaze of her family, is able to get into all sorts of mischief. The very act of negotiating a way in the world is meant to instill such notions in women. Female independence might, indeed, allow the play of untrammelled or at least autonomous sexuality. She thus needs to be controlled. A neighbour's first suspicion is that Chinu has eloped, bringing intense shame to the family.

> GIRIN. To perdition, I tell you: that entire family'll go to perdition. I'm sure that girl's eloped with someone. That's it, she's eloped.

His young granddaughter remonstrates with him, in fact tries to persuade him that this is not true.

> LILY. Really, Granddad, don't you know Auntie Chinu? Haven't you seen her from when she was about this high? Is she the sort to elope?

She is told to shut up by her grandparents. Her grandmother then makes a pointed observation.

> GIRIN'S WIFE (*to Girin*). You know, there's something very fishy about all this. One can't really trust these working-girl types, can one?

> GIRIN. Well, that's what happens when women stop acting like women.

> LILY. Really? And what about when women have to go out to work like men?

She is again told to shut up, of course. Here is the voice of orthodox wisdom in its incarnation as moral authority. It is the voice of suspicion, of control. And it is not exclusive to the male gender, either. Girin's wife is part of the system and has as little faith in the working woman as her husband. Nor, one presumes, does she have any trouble in accepting the idea that working is somehow unwomanly. But in a sense, it is not the elderly conservatives who are the real issue, but the extent to which their ideas are consciously or subconsciously shared by those who otherwise reject their narrow-minded bigotry. Lily, their grandchild, clearly rejects their opinions regarding Chinu's morals, or the lack thereof. But she shares the feeling of social opprobrium which elopement engenders- 'Is she the sort to elope?' What is important to remember is that this comment is made in defence of Chinu. Lily is obviously convinced that Chinu is incapable of compromising her family's honour. But what elopement consists of is a declaration—however fearful—of one's autonomy; of choosing one's partner even if one has to flee, in order to escape some form of retribution. Retribution, because this form of choice is seen to besmirch the family's honour. And it is at this level, of honour, or more accurately, respectability, that several of Chinu's family are inevitably drawn to voice their concerns—especially as the period of absence becomes ever longer.

But it is precisely during this demonstration of shared concern for social face that individual vulnerability and tensions are highlighted; moreover, the fault lines within the family are sharply delineated. In choosing to believe that Chinu might be dead, their fears of being cast adrift in economic turmoil are merged with the normal feelings of terror at the thought of losing a family member. But in choosing to believe that she may perhaps be alive, their outrage at the possibility of the loss of respectability only serves to remind them how they have all contributed to this situation. They even turn on each other in their recriminations. The one who binds the family has contributed to the fracturing of the family facade.

Chinu herself is acutely aware of the fragility of her position. Greeted by a stony-faced silence upon her return home, she tells Minu, 'Didn't you people want me to return home ... Did you consider that I might have something to say for myself? [...] D'you people really trust me so very little? Of course, if I'd had an accident you'd have had nothing to say ...' By now, the crust has worn very thin indeed.

Not so in the case of Sasank, retired professor, husband and father of three, who abandons home and family one wild and stormy night. His is a life which reveals itself to have been arid in the extreme, with the exception of his closeness to his elder daughter. A man who remains true to his own personal moral codes, Sasank's life is a saga of estrangement from his family, as well as his colleagues. Even worse, his adherence to his own beliefs is seen by those around him as a manifestation of his lack of drive, rather than for what it is, a disinclination to compromise. The only one who is willing to see this is his daughter Neeta. Early in the film, we see the family discussing Sasank's attitude.

SUDHA. Well, who's to explain it to him? He just sits in his room all day and broods . . . Oh, I don't know . . .

Camera moves a fraction to show Seema entering. She joins the others at the table.

SEEMA. What d'you mean you don't know? Nobody forced him to sit at home, did they? He's lost interest in teaching; he says so himself.

SUDHA. Yes. And look at some of his older colleagues. They've had their jobs extended by five to six years, and still don't want to retire. They just keep on teaching . . .

Neeta's face has been growing increasingly stormy as this conversation carries on. She seems almost near to tears.

NEETA. They keep on teaching and Father doesn't, is that right? . . . The things you say . . .

Neeta rises and rushes off towards the door, screen right. She pauses at the door and turns towards the others. Only Seema can be seen, however, sitting screen right. Neeta looks as though she is suppressing her tears with the greatest difficulty.

NEETA. Is Baba the sort that sits idle, really? Don't you notice how he pores over his books all day?'

Estranged from a family who neither understand him, nor have any sympathy for what he stands for, Sasank has 'gone missing', i.e., retreated into his own world, for some time. Finally, he absents himself completely, by walking out one stormy night. But from the after-effects of this disappearance we would hardly surmise that Sasank's presence was as tenuous as had been imagined. The shock waves not only disrupt the family's life; The family also discovers that it is in some ways to be continually reminded of Sasank's absence. The bank, for instance, will not let them touch the money in Sasank's account for a period of seven years, money that they badly need. They perceive that they are not really able to take care of his large collection of books, books that in certain ways exemplify Sasank's troubled relationship with his wife and two younger children. This library of books will, in due course, concern us once more. As for his family, they are forced to confront the fact that not only is their past not necessarily comprehensible to them in their own terms, but that some of it is also missing. Their only solution is to reconstruct, however painfully, their relationship to the absent Sasank. In the process, they discover things that were best left unknown, including the most damning of all, that they might well have rather badly misjudged the missing man.

All three families are, thus, badly haunted by the past, but in significantly different ways. The family in *Ekdin Achanak* has to learn to cope with a past that is personal. It is the complex network of their own past relationships that has to be uncovered. In the case of the other two, however, it is the socially shared past, the historical past, that affects them, as much as their personal and family pasts. Yet a sharp distinction has to be drawn between the past as history and the historical past as perceived by these people. For the protagonists of both *Kharij* as well as *Ekdin Pratidin* live oblivious of the past. They are entirely concentrated in their attempts to cope with the present. They are not only quite ignorant of the historical past, no matter in how recent a time, but are also unconcerned about their own past. And yet, the past has seeped into them, so to speak, it is part of their very being. The family in *Ekdin Pratidin* provides a good example. In going out to work,

Chinu, the oldest daughter, stands squarely in line with current trends. She is educated and enjoys a certain degree of autonomy. Yet, she is very much the dutiful and obedient daughter. And not merely in her caretaking and nurturing qualities. We know, for instance, that she has never been out late before; this is the principal reason that the family is so agitated in the first place. And indeed, we learn that she may well have given up her chance at happiness because of her family. She was in love with a young man whom her parents, especially Mother, considered a poor prospect. The young man was shot dead by the police, but it is eminently clear that Chinu's family would never have approved of the marriage. The second daughter, Minu, accuses her mother of precisely that, i.e., of never considering Chinu's needs. This takes place during an emotion-choked and heated exchange. Mother has earlier strenuously denied that she had no intention of arranging Chinu's marriage.

> MOTHER (*angrily*). Now what's got into you today, Minu? Are you going to tell me that you don't know I've been collecting her wedding ornaments over the years?

As the camera pans over the faces in the room, the following voices are headed.

> MINU (*off-screen*). But didi never wanted all that. All she wanted was to marry Somnathda.
>
> MOTHER (*off-screen*). And a fine state she'd have been in, if that marriage had taken place.
>
> MINU (*off-screen*). But at least she'd have been fulfilled.
>
> MOTHER (*off-screen*). Fulfilled, is it? And spent her entire life in widow's weeds!
>
> MINU (*off-screen*). Of course, if Somnathda hadn't been in that state, you'd have arranged her marriage with him, wouldn't you?
>
> MOTHER. He didn't even have a roof over his head. He used to spend all his time working for the Party. And he wanted Chinu to earn a living.

MINU. She's doing exactly that even now, Ma!

Nevertheless, the past has, of course, seeped into their very bones, even if the people concerned are unaware of it. It may be said that they are unaware of it precisely to the extent that it has been imperceptibly integrated into their social beings. But when their lives are thrown into turmoil due to some upheaval, we are able to see their present being underscored by an irruption of the past in its midst. In other words, by our common history manifesting itself in the family's own history. Mother's continuing rejection of Somnath as a possible husband for her daughter even now, several years after his death, highlights this process. She simultaneously finds Somnath unacceptable because he is not modern enough, in her instrumentalist acceptance of the term, whilst rejecting him because he has entirely, too completely, internalized certain crucial aspects of modernism. Somnath is good enough because '[h] e didn't even have a roof over his head' and because he '... used to spend all his time working for the Party.' In other words, not only was Somnath poor, but he had no prospects, especially in the vital career market. He was not a yuppie, and had no ambition to be one. Yet his total rejection of this arche-symbol of recent modern social striving—how much more resonant it seems these days—entailed his equally wholehearted acceptance of an even more pertinently modern career, that of a full-time political worker.

Moreover, in Somnath we have a representative of the historical past come crashing into individual lives. We have learned earlier on that Somnath, who was shot dead by the police during a demonstration, was a Naxalite. One of those young men and women who spread out from the urban areas into the countryside, in order to organize a peasant-based guerrilla movement, whilst simultaneously attempting to engage in cultural and political insurgency in the urban areas. Debates regarding the nature of their 'left-adventurist' politics can continue, but most people are aware that the very flower of an entire generation of youth was cut down in the process. As a young man espousing such politics, it was hardly surprising for Somnath to have wanted Chinu to earn a living. And it is precisely on this espousal that Mother finds him wanting as a prospective son-in-law. In her world, men take care of women as part of the natural order of things. Unfortunately, in the same order of things, (unmarried) daughters take care of their families. Which raises more than a few problems to be faced, as the film shows us.

Living so intensely in their personal time whilst simultaneously being unmindful of their shared times, seems to seal them off from one another. They are often unaware of what is transpiring under their very noses. And this quality of being unmindful makes them seem indifferent to one another; their behaviour seems entirely self-centred, and even selfish. Until, of course, circumstances intervene. Mother is a particular focus of this indifference. Significantly, she is the one person whose labour is taken for granted to the point of being unnoticed. What is more, that she subsumes herself entirely to her family's needs is not only seen as entirely normative, but as something that deserves no acknowledgement. It is, after all, her duty. In a sense both she and Chinu are in the same position, in that both are sacrifices to the greater needs of the family and are equally overlooked. Chinu is, of course, her mother's somewhat more fulfilled image, particularly because she has achieved that degree of autonomy which is entirely outside Mother's limits of possibility. Moreover, she is the nurturer now, as Mother has, presumably, been in the past. Mother has now been reduced to the state of caretaker, of course. Yet both share this similarity; that for all the contributions they make, they are easily relegated to the status of failures. They are seen as individuals who have failed to discharge their responsibilities. There are rumblings regarding Chinu throughout the film, which come to a head at the denouement. But Mother is charged early. From the beginning, our impression of Mother is that she is engaged in some household chore or the other. Generally unaided, it goes without saying! On one of the first occasions that we see Mother not engaged in some task, she is in a state of some exhaustion, but is thought to be idling. The camera has followed Hrishikesh into the bedroom.

The camera pans to show the bedroom through the bars of a window. Mother is on the far side of the room, looking tired and forlorn. Hrishikesh enters and sits on the bed, his back to the camera. Cut to mid-close-up of Mother, who can now be seen in a state of virtual exhaustion, then cut back, to Hrishikesh, sitting on the bed. Poltu can be seen lying behind him.

HRISHIKESH: Perhaps she's gone to Srirampur, to visit your sister.

MOTHER. She'll never visit a relative.

Cut to a high angle shot of Jhunu and Poltu sleeping on the bed.

HRISHIKESH: Now Jhunu's fallen asleep as well. Jhunu . . . Jhunu!

JHUNU: I'm not asleep.

MOTHER. You will be in a minute, though. Why don't you go and have your dinner?

JHUNU: I'm just going . . .

MOTHER. Never mind this just going business. Go and eat, it's quite late. And put your father's dinner out as well: I'm feeling very tired, I can't manage any more . . . Well? Jhunu . . . Jhunu!

JHUNU: What is it?

MOTHER. Go and eat your dinner. Go and wash your face, then eat.

Jhunu sits up on the bed, her back to the camera.

JHUNU: Why don't you put the dinner out?

MOTHER. You mean you can't help yourself one day? What d'you take me for?

Camera zooms very slightly.

JHUNU: Well, you're just sitting there!

Cut. Jhunu crosses in extreme close-up and leaves frame, screen right. Mother is now seen in mid-close-up. She looks very angry.

MOTHER. I'm just sitting, am I? Perhaps it's because I can barely manage to stand.

Cut. Minu appears at the bedroom door. Jhunu crosses her and then stops.

MINU. What's going on here?

JHUNU: Just look at Ma, Mejdi. She's snapping my head off for no reason at all.

MINU. Yes, so I've noticed all evening.

It goes without saying that Mother reacts angrily to this blatant unfairness. But even in her rage she is reduced to impotence, for no one, not even her husband Hrishikesh, takes much note of her anger, much less sympathizes with her. Hrishikesh and both daughters simply leave the room. But that is of minor importance.

What this sequence reveals about Mother is the way she is perceived. Or rather, how certain areas of her existence are not perceived, for not one person seems to have noticed what Mother has been doing all day. This quality of unmindfulness comes, as I have said, from living in a manner which makes them indifferent to their shared time, making them seemingly indifferent towards one another. Seemingly, because every so often, crises—large or small remind them of their mutuality and bonds. As at the very start of the film, when young Poltu returns home with a head injury.

Nevertheless, the general tenor is one of an inclination to overlook each other's circumstances, locked as they are into their own. Part of it is the result of living a life at the bare edges of survival; after all, if the oldest daughter disappears, or even loses her job, this family is sunk. Each man unto himself is a familiar, though certainly not automatic, response in such circumstances. And indeed, Mother herself gives vent to such feelings by complaining that Chinu's disappearance would scuttle the family. This is not sufficient to explain the response to Mother's role. In Jhunu's case, it may be argued that her behaviour is that of a stereotypical teenager. But how has even Minu, who functions both as a clear-eyed and unsentimental observer and as an unofficial conscience carrier, entirely managed to overlook Mother's daily drudgery? The answer must surely be that she has not. Like everyone else in the family, she sees this as Mother's normative function and thus has no reason to give it any special weight. Like several other things, Mother's daily chores have become 'absent' because they are not part of anyone's consciousness, except her own. In fact, Mother has become the personification of her daily routines; she has little existence other than them. This is underscored when we discover that after getting her job, Chinu decided to buy various members of her family—on their demand—such things as musical instruments and clothes. She further ensured that her younger sister Minu's workload was reduced. But for her mother, her present was to be a new stove. Not that a new stove was not needed. But her job as a dutiful daughter is to streamline her mother's chores. Mother's identification with housework is complete.

This, of course, parallels Chinu's own fate, which is to be identified with her status of principal, or, rather, only, breadwinner for her family. Her position, that of the dutiful daughter, too, is interpreted as normative. And no thought is given to the psychological costs that Chinu has paid for discharging her duty in such exemplary fashion. The fierce attention to the present enables these people—like so many other families—to obliterate their past. Both their individual pasts as well as their collective pasts.

Yet, despite this, we do know that they have pasts, individual, shared and collective. Not only that, but the building they live in, its owner, not only has a past, but we are told of it. Thus, they have—the main protagonists—a background, which is acknowledged, even if through the device of an invisible narrator. Thus, we know that Chinu's father came to live in this building—from where?—twenty-three years ago, with his wife and the two-year-old Chinu, and that in the intervening years, the family has grown rather dramatically. We know that he had retired from a job with a minimal pension—enough 'to pay the rent and for a few sundries'. We not only know that Dwarik Mullick is the scion of an old land-owning family but that he is a man with pretensions: 'His forefathers used to spend their time ruling their subjects and racing pigeons. His blood retains some traces of its previous aristocratic hauteur.' Moreover, he is a man who 'certainly cannot be accused of being overfond of his tenants.' These 'wretched creatures' most definitely do not share his aristocratic past. Similarly, we know that the building dates back to 1857, '. . . the year of the Indian Mutiny. The year in which this house was built by Babu Nabin Chandra Mullick.' Even the city, Calcutta, where the action is situated, has a past, articulated by both the narrator, as well as the protagonists, even if the details highlighted are somewhat misleading, to say nothing of being unfair. There is more to Calcutta than a narrative 'replete with meetings, processions, riots, bloodshed, famines and the occasional war'. And it is this common time, this shared time, which allows this family to overcome—to however limited a degree—their greatest social crisis, Chinu's return home in the early hours of the morning. For a while, at least, they are acutely sensitive to each other and the ties that bind them together, something that is not really possible without remembering their mutual past.

The final altercation with their landlord Dwarik is predicated on his acute consciousness of the tension between his aristocratic past and plebeian present. He can only survive this by examining all social behaviour in terms of 'respectability'. And Chinu's family have earlier examined respectability from their shared past, i.e., their family history, and found it somewhat wanting. Chinu has had occasion to remind them on her return, that the choice between respectability and her safety has been fraught, on both sides of the equation.

Cut to the girls' bedroom. Minu is huddled on bed, staring studiously at the floor. Chinu comes close to her, looking at her sister with a hurt expression.

CHINU: What is it, Minu? Didn't you people want me to return home? [...] Did you consider that I might have something to say for myself ... D'you people really trust me so very little? Of course, if I'd had an accident you'd have had nothing to say ...

Minu is sharply reminded of the costs, personal and collective, that have had to be paid in order to maintain this mask, even if it is wearing threadbare. And earlier, it is, of course, Minu herself who has rather brutally reminded her family of the state of their lives.

Cut to Hrishikesh in close-up. The camera pulls back until Hrishikesh is seen in mid-shot. Minu walks into the room from screen right and sits on a chair. The camera pans and then tilts right to show Mother sitting on the floor, her back propped against the bed. She is quietly dozing.

Cut to mid-shot of Hrishikesh.

HRISHIKESH: God only knows what's happened to the girl!
MOTHER. Minu didn't she tell you anything at all before she left? Come on love, don't keep secrets from me?
MINU. For goodness' sake, Ma! Why would I want to keep any secrets from you?
MOTHER. I just know she's never coming back.
MINU. Well, if you know so much, shut up about it.
HRISHIKESH: Minu!!

Cut to Topu, seen in a slight high angle shot.

MINU (*off-screen*). Dada, I believe you threw up after you visited the morgue. Amalda told me you threw up.

Cut to a close-up of Minu. The loud ticking of the clock can be heard.

MINU. . . . Tell me, haven't you felt like puking when you see *this* morgue? This room? This house?

This is where Mother's comment about Chinu scuttling the family comes in.

MINU. Yes, that's what's really important to us, isn't it? That we've, been cast adrift. A girl's been suffocating little by little every day, in this house. And today . . . we're all thinking about her a lot, aren't we?

And towards the end of the sequence, we hear Mother's *cri de coeur* for the first time.

MOTHER.. Why're you telling me all this? Tell that man over there, that man sitting so silently [. . .] The only thing he's ever done, is to remain silent; and left all the responsibilities to me . . .

Mother slowly dissolves in tears and slumps to the floor.

Cut to close-up of Topu, grimly looking away from everyone else. Cut to close-up of Hrishikesh. He slowly stands up in the midst of this emotionally exhausted group, then silently walks out into the courtyard. A high angle shot of Hrishikesh, standing alone in the middle of a dark courtyard:

Thus, when Dwarik Mullick, the landlord, comments about Chinu being 'disreputable', without knowing it, he highlights the costs of maintaining a reputation. Moreover, he inadvertently hits Chinu's family's sorest point: their guilt regarding failures of individual and collective responsibility, their exploitation of one member of the family, their impotence in the face of overwhelming pressures, the way their, indifference towards one another has isolated them from each other, and so on. But it is precisely this point that helps them to come together and defend Chinu, if necessary, by application of force. In so doing, they defend themselves as a group. This is, of course, the point where *Ekdin*—one day, in Bengali—ends.

After this is the closing sequence, where what we see is *Pratidin*.[3] It is morning, and the daily routine of the inhabitants of the building on Nabin Chandra Lane has started, all over again. And in this flurry of shots, we see Mother in the kitchen, obscured by the smoke from a coal stove. She looks weighed down by the weight of the world. And yet she has started all over again; her day is once more beginning. The night-long absence of the elder daughter and the catharsis of defending her against social opprobrium, has helped them to garner their resources and get on with the simple business of survival. In order to achieve this, they have been forced to shed their routine posture of indifference towards one another.

We see a similar dialectic unfold in another of the three films, *Ekdin Achanak*. This is a film whose basic logic is almost entirely given over to an examination of the past. The principal characters spend their energies rummaging in their pasts—individual as well as familial—as well as sometimes attempting to excavate the past carefully, in order to reconstruct it. In the process, painful and disconcerting as it is, they gather the strength and material for facing the future, together. There are, of course, many differences between Sasank's family and Chinu's, even though the soul searching is precipitated by roughly a similar cause, i.e., Sasank's abrupt departure from home. This fact is in itself a big difference between the two cases, for Sasank, unlike Chinu, has disappeared permanently. Moreover, the former's is a middle-class family, who own their own home; their oldest daughter works, but has a better job. She also has a man friend, though here, too, the possibilities for the future, it is hinted, are limited. The son is attempting to establish a business, they have successful—even rich—relatives, as well as modestly successful friends. Sasank himself has been a college professor, and, possibly, a brilliant academic among mediocre colleagues. Nor is the financial state of the family he has so suddenly abandoned anywhere near as parlous as Chinu's family's. Moreover, unlike the other family, this one is anything but oblivious to the past. Which is as it should be, given the logic driving the narrative.

All such, and numerous other differences notwithstanding, it is the one great similarity which is of crucial significance. Like Chinu's family, these individuals not only have a past, but we are made aware of it. For instance, we not only surmise that Sasank was an academic, from the book-lined study and his general demeanour, but later learn that he comes from a family of academics. The books and the family are, indeed, linked. This is made clear in the sequence where Sasank's student, Aparna, has dropped in unannounced. Sasank has asked her to enter.

Cut to close-up of Aparna. The camera then moves back to show Arun standing behind Aparna. Seema is at the door.

APARNA. I'm not alone, though.

SEEMA. Uncle Arun . . .

Arun and Aparna enter Sasank's study where Aparna is to be seen examining Sasank's books whilst Arun sits at Sasank's desk.

SASANK (*off screen, to Aparna*). You just turn up, without even informing me . . .

APARNA. I wanted to surprise you . . . Your library is quite fantastic.

Then Sasank enters and sits on the chair behind the desk.

SASANK. They're almost all my father's books. I haven't been able to increase the collection by much . . . Have you noticed the indexing? Even that was done by my father.

APARNA. Fabulous!

It is later in the same sequence that we learn what makes Sasank so awkward. His friend Arun is trying to convince Sasank to join him in a business venture.

ARUN. Listen, can I finish what I came to tell you? I'm in a bit of a hurry.

SASANK. You're always dying to leave within minutes of arriving.

Aparna gets up and goes to the far corner of the room, where she starts looking at the books once again.

SUDHA. Not everyone's like you, you know. Some people work.

SASANK. Did you hear that? It's her perennial complaint.

ARUN. I've had a scheme in my head for a long time. Now, I've finally made it a reality. I've opened a 'Tutorial Home'.

SASANK. Oh . . . wonderful.

Cut to mid-close-up of Aparna. She looks up from the book she has been examining in some astonishment, at hearing Sasank's comment.

Cut to mid-close-up of Arun looking earnestly at a disinterested Sasank.

Cut to a composite shot, with a disgusted Sudha and an amused Aparna listening in to the conversation.

ARUN. You'll have to do more than merely congratulate me. I want you to teach there.

SASANK. Teach? Who, me? In a 'Tutorial Home'?

ARUN. Now don't you say no. Bhabhi, you tell him. It's only an hour a day and in the evenings, at that. They're all B.A. students, in their final year.

SASANK. Listen, who's going to do the teaching? Is it me or Bhabhi? What're you convincing her for, eh?

Aparna smiles tongue-in-cheek.

ARUN. It's not as if you can't spare the time, is it? You're sitting at home all day.

SASANK (*to Sudha*). You liked that bit, didn't you? Sitting at home . . . (*To Arun, laughingly*) That's what they all say, sitting at home . . .

Sasank and Arun argue for a while, but Sasank makes it clear that teaching in a 'Tutorial Home' is not for him, even though he feels that he is able to write better 'notes' than those generally available in the market. His wife Sudha now turns to Aparna and asks her to intervene.

> APARNA. The thing is . . . I don't think Sir's capable of doing something like that.
>
> SASANK. That is true. I think it's beyond me. I proved to be a bad teacher. Bad . . . ! Very bad . . . !!

This one sequence tells us much about the protagonists. Something of their past, as well as their personal attitudes and inclinations. Sasank's intransigence, his disinclination to do what he considers demeaning intellectual labour ('Who, me? In a "Tutorial Home"?'), his arrogance ('I proved to be a bad teacher', etc.), his wife Sudha's disinclination to see his attitude as anything other than patronizing superiority—a feeling that a large section of the family shares for example. Throughout, we keep learning more about these people and their past. And it is precisely this understanding that helps the various protagonists to come together in the end as a family group. This is despite the fact that their primary interest has not been in reconstructing the past *per se*. They have simply been interested in working out, for the sake of their own satisfaction, why Sasank might have abandoned his family in so abrupt a manner. Though they are not successful in discovering why, they manage to learn something about him and about themselves. During this process, they manage, amongst other things, to let go of the past. We see this in the penultimate sequence, when the family takes the step of donating Sasank's beloved collection of books to his college. All along, they had been hanging on to the books, neither being able to look after them, nor able to get rid of them. This is much like their relationship to the memory of the absent Sasank. By giving the books away for housing, they have been able to start making peace with their own ambivalent feelings about the absent Sasank. They are able to realize that they may have been wrong about the past, and that they now have something to face the future with. More, they are able to acknowledge to each other that they may have misread Sasank. The film ends as it began, on a wild and stormy night, with a group of people sitting together. Only this time, because they can regret their own misjudgements about the absent man, they may be said to have grown.

It is instructive to compare the family in the remaining film, *Kharij*, with the other two. If *Ekdin Achanak* is a film about a family's attempt to excavate the past, *Kharij* is a film about a family that seems to have no past. They live entirely in the present. In fact, unlike the families in the other two films, this family—a nuclear family which starts as a couple in the establishing shot itself and then expands to include one son—seems to have no relatives, either. Not a little surprising, in the Indian context. They are archetypal modern city dwellers, isolated to themselves, with only a handful of friends and acquaintances. After all, no one cares who you are in the big city, or indeed, where you come from. Throughout the film, we never find out anything about their pasts, who they are, where they have come from, what their previous experiences were. What we know of them is that this young couple, Anjan and Mamata, have one another and that their eyes are firmly fixed on the future. Being so future-oriented is, of course, entirely appropriate for a young couple with such strong aspirations of social mobility. They are the representatives of India's new class of urban consumers. That such people should be deracinated from all save their narrow urban milieu should come as no surprise, given their desire for social climbing. They—especially Anjan, the husband, which again should come as no surprise—are also people who derive both status as well as satisfaction from possessions and have no hesitation in seeing other people in instrumental terms. This becomes clear from the first couple of sequences. The opening sequence takes place inside a taxi:

> A man's voice is heard, hailing a taxi. Cut to interior of cab; driver's upper body is visible, from the back. A couple are having a conversation off-screen, while the street can be seen through the windowscreen.

ANJAN. Well then?

MAMATA. Well then, what?

ANJAN. After our marriage . . . ?

MAMATA. Hmm?

ANJAN. What would you like?

MAMATA. What would I like?

ANJAN. Your own flat? A car?

MAMATA. No. . .

ANJAN. Only sarees?

MAMATA. No, no, no.

ANJAN. Fridge?

MAMATA. Oh, no.

ANJAN. TV?

MAMATA. Not even that.

ANJAN. Well, you tell me.

MAMATA. You don't know?

ANJAN. No.

MAMATA. You mean you really don't know?

ANJAN. No. You tell me.

MAMATA. Mister, I only want you. (*Both laugh.*)

The driver turns abruptly, and looks over his left shoulder, and the shot freezes at this point.

Already it becomes clear that not only is Anjan's idea of giving restricted to material things, but to objects that, in his world, clearly possess status value. It needs to be stressed that this is not a yuppie couple in any real sense, in that they have barely entered the initial stage of that particular social journey. One is hardly a yuppie without owning a home and a car. Nevertheless, Anjan certainly wants to get there. It is also clear that Mamata is much more capable of being tender-minded and romantic; in a word, 'sentimental'. It also provides the first faint hint that Anjan sees Mamata's role as provider of tender loving care and his as provider of material well-being.

This, as well as his instrumental view of people, is underscored in the very next sequence.

Cut to the interior of a room. A man in his early 30s is shaving in front of a mirror, with an orange towel draped over his shoulders. He is seen from the back; little is visible of his face, which is covered with lather. He sounds like the man in the taxi and seems a smug sort of person, obviously quite pleased with himself. A man who hopes to be moving up in the world.

ANJAN. You landed your job just before we got married, whilst I got a promotion within two years. It was your luck, and my efficiency. Now tell me what you'd like? Your own flat?

Anjan carries on listing the various things that his wife might desire but Mamata explains that what is required is a servant.

MAMATA. No, dear. (*As she goes to the table*) What I really need now is a servant; preferably a boy not more than twelve to fourteen years old.

Mamata gives her son a glass of milk.

ANJAN (*off-screen*). Low salary . . .

MAMATA. Don't spill it on your shirt, love.

ANJAN (*off-screen*). Won't eat much . . .

MAMATA. Yes. (*Laughs.*)

ANJAN (*off-screen*). And won't talk back . . .

MAMATA. Besides, he'll fetch the coal, light the stove, make the tea . . . (*To her son*) Pupai, here love, let me; come and sit here. (*To Anjan*) . . . He'll learn how to make tea (*starts doing the bed*) wash the tea things . . .

ANJAN (*off-screen*). Fetch cigarettes and matches . . .

MAMATA. Yes, and run small errands, do the dusting . . . go to the shops, queue for the kerosene, go to the *dhobi* . . .

ANJAN (*off-screen*). And lose a few clothes in the process.

MAMATA. Look after the house whilst we're at work . . . play with Pupai.

Mamata goes up to Pupal and sitting in front of him, hangs a canteen of water from a strap over his shoulder.

MAMATA. . . . And what else will he do for my darling Pupai? He'll take him to school.

PUPAI: And bring me back . . . ?

Freezing shot of a smiling Mamata.

As this sequence shows, despite their strong areas of identity, the differences in attitude between husband and wife are considerable. Anjan is not merely happily smug and self-satisfied. His perspective on the matter of hiring a servant is very different from his wife's. Even though asked in a humorous manner, it is noteworthy that his initial comments are in what might be called, somewhat tongue-in-cheek, the abstract and managerial mode. That is to say, he stresses—however jokingly—the principle of maximal returns for minimal investment: i.e., low salary, a small appetite and not cheeky to boot. These might well be thought to be the qualities of a 'disciplined' labour force. Mamata's is, on the other hand, a much more human response. Her's is a simple listing of the jobs that a housewife, especially a working mother, wants done. Nevertheless, her expectations are quite remarkable, particularly from a twelve-year-old boy. Nor is little Pupai without his expectations. Nonetheless, the wife's more 'normal' response is indicative not only of the differences in their temperaments, but will have an effect on their relationship.

It is Anjan who is most severely examined in the course of the film. But although he is definitely intended to be seen as the representative of his class of people, there are several others, much like him in attitude. Interestingly enough, all of them, like Anjan, are individuals who seem to have no past. In order to know that a person has a past, we need to hear of some incident from it, or be told of an individual who was part of it, or learn how it affects the present in some way and so on. But we know nothing of these people in the period before the events of the film. They are all victims of some strange amnesia, both about themselves and the greater world they live in. The only way we gather information about the passing of time in the case of Anjan and Mamata, is by inference, i.e., from the changes in their environment; otherwise, everything seems pitched squarely in the present tense. From the first sequence, we infer that they are about to be married; from the second, that about eight years or more have passed, because of the presence of a six- or seven-year-old child. And the only bits of concrete information that we get are that Anjan was promoted within two years of his marriage and that Mamata got her job just before marriage. Otherwise, virtually everything that happens in the film takes place in the here and now. One consequence of this amnesia—can they really not have a past? —is that, not seeming to have any common memories of the world they share, not even discussing past events, they behave as though they have no responsibilities towards anyone other than themselves or their own. Even their idea of shared space, social or moral, does not extend beyond the narrowest confines.

This incapacity to visualize a world which is larger than the limits set by the narrowest and most parochial concepts of social and individual functioning, a sort of 'me, myself, mine' version of functioning, so to speak, extends to the pettiest of matters. Say for instance, the putting out of rubbish:

> Cut to the stairs, where an elderly man is seen ascending. He is well protected against the cold, and is carrying a stick. He stops at the landing. This is the landlord, Benoy Lahiri. […] Benoy starts up the stairs again. Hari is coming down the stairs with a bucket full of garbage. Benoy stops Hari.
>
> BENOY. Hey you, don't you dare leave the rubbish in the middle of the pavement. Why can't you put it on one side? It's almost become impossible to walk on the pavement these days.

It is difficult to believe that such individuals can be part of a modern urban setting, though some might say that 'contemporary' is more accurate a description than 'modern'. It is clear that Benoy has no hesitation in appropriating public space for personal convenience, while, at the same time, complaining vociferously about the misuse of the said space. He lacks the ability to relate his own actions and attitudes to the greater whole.

This inability (perhaps disinclination would be a kinder formulation) to own responsibility to anything or anyone outside one's narrowly defined circle marks Anjan just as strongly. His lack of any interest in people not of his immediate concern, thus, not only allows him to attempt to elide over the glaringly obvious, but, if that fails, to brush it aside with words. He is a devotee of the expedient. Thus, when Mamata, whilst hiring Palan for the job, tells his father that she will provide the boy's bedthings, but what of warm clothes? (the very idea of having warm clothes seems to startle Haran, the boy's father), Anjan immediately intervenes, saying they'll take care of it, and she should hire him. Anjan simply wants the job done, without concerning himself overmuch with his desires or promises. Nor, we presume, did he have any great ambition to fulfil his promises, since after Palan's death it becomes clear that the boy had no warm clothes nor, indeed, any adequate protection against the cold. It is also clear that Anjan felt no concern about an eleven-year-old child sleeping under the stairs. This is not to suggest that Anjan is some sort of evil, or even cruel person. Nor, indeed, that Mamata is significantly more caring or socially conscious than he is. But what sets Anjan apart is his disinterest. His perception seems to be that he provides for the family and the rest is up to others. His job is to ensure that Mamata has a servant. To the rest, including the state of the said servant's existence, he remains sublimely indifferent. Having brought home the bacon, so to speak, he expects his world to function in a suitably cozy fashion. Moreover, he certainly does not intend to examine this world too closely. That might be too revelatory for comfort, especially in terms of consequences of (in)actions.

Unfortunately, if there is an area that consequences directly bear upon, it is that of responsibilities. Therefore, responsibilities can sometimes become impossible to shrug off. Not only do the consequences of one's actions, like the proverbial chickens, come home to roost, but they are sometimes overwhelming and leave one bereft of even the strength to manage denial. This is partly because of the onrush of guilt and partly due to the fear of further consequences. This is exactly what the discovery of the young boy's corpse sets in motion. The problem that Anjan and Co. have, of course, is that they lack any sophisticated mechanism for facing up to responsibility, given that by definition consequences can only follow actions; their amnesia and their willful existence in the endless present results in their actions being erased. They cannot bear responsibility when they have nothing to be responsible for, as they have no idea what it is they are being held responsible for. The only thing they have to face is the consequences of their actions. And given that this can only take place in the immediate present, they can only react. The combination of guilt and fear ensures that the usual reaction is to find fault; in other words, hold someone else to blame. Each and every time that the consequences of their actions, or inaction, have to be confronted, someone has to be found to shoulder the blame. As, for instance, when Mamata blurts out to the police inspector that she had last entered the kitchen at 10.30 p.m. to leave a pan of water simmering on the coal stove. The inspector is astonished that someone would leave a pan simmering on a coal stove in the same room as a little boy. Anjan is furious with her when they are alone.

ANJAN. You needn't have told them about it.

MAMATA. About what?

ANJAN. The business about the stove—that you hadn't put it out. It wasn't necessary at all.

MAMATA. Why, did they say anything about it?

ANJAN. What could they say? You'd already said everything that there was to say.

MAMATA. But I do that every day.

ANJAN. But he didn't sleep there every day. Didn't you notice how they were peering inside the pans?

MAMATA (*as she prepares to sit on the bed*). But that's the water I boil every day for the washing. In any case, what would you have liked me to say? That I carefully put the stove out? Or perhaps that I had fed Palan before going to bed?

This propensity to hold someone responsible shows itself throughout the film. And it is shared by one and all. The landlord· Benoy Lahiri, is the person who most clearly articulates this rejection of any personal responsibility during a sharp argument with Anjan. He has earlier been quizzed by the police as to why there is no form of ventilation provided in the room where the dead boy has been found. Lahiri answers by saying that ventilation was not felt to be necessary because it was only a kitchen. Later he remonstrates with Anjan in the presence of Mamata and Sreela for inviting some local youths in. Anjan, it goes without saying, instantly denies having done so, much to Mamata and Sreela's surprise.

ANJAN. . . . And even if I did, what of it? Have we committed a theft? Anyway, you could have come down once; it is your house, after all; you do have some responsibilities, or don't you?'

BENOY. Responsibilities? What responsibilities? I've rented the house out, and that's all. That's where it ends.

Their denial of any past, or collective, time, actually acts as an impediment to these people realizing that they have, all of them, to greater or lesser degrees, contributed to the child's death. Simultaneously, their guilt and fear makes them attempt to seek someone else to blame, whilst remaining suspicious of everyone else's motives. Thus, if Anjan seeks legal advice, so does Benoy. Each hopes to hear that there is some way in which the other can be held at fault. At the cremation ground, where it is obvious that Anjan is under no threat at all, the first question that Sreela's grandfather asks him is whether he has had any problems. He means, of course, from Palan's grieving friends and relatives.

Denial of any responsibility and vision of the past makes these people vulnerable to guilt and leaves them unable to cope with their present. For it is precisely through their present that the past manifests itself. In the gap left behind by the absent Palan, we catch glimpses of the shared past—history—that people like Anjan deny. And not only through the agency of Palan's absence. For the boy's very existence in Anjan and Mamata's household is an indication of those glaring deficiencies in village life that have forced his family to send him away in the first place: the absence of good jobs and any real prospects for the future. We notice this from his very arrival at their door, as Palan's father explains why the boy is being put into service.

> HARAN. Oh no, I'm sure he'll be very happy with you. Ganesh, from next door, has explained everything. We're from the same village, you see [. . .] There's a famine back home—we've had a severe drought, you know . . . Because he'll be living with you, he'll be getting two square meals, not to mention a salary. As for the work, you've just got to teach him. He's a village lad after all; he can do any kind of work. He'll even carry heavy loads from downstairs—you only have to tell him.

This one exchange lays bare the nature of village life in parts of India. What is revealing is not so much what life is like under conditions of extreme stress—severe drought and famine—but what the normative expectations of life are, in the village. Through the agency of this boy's history, we can infer the dynamics which drive the millions of child labourers of India to seek work outside their villages. A few scenes later, Haran makes this even clearer:

> HARAN. Won't you increase it by a few more rupees at least? He's only a little boy after all, without a mother . . . And if they didn't need the money very badly, would anyone . . . ?

As this defeated parent suggests, people put their young children out to work because they need the money, desperately. The irony of this particular exchange is that whilst Haran is putting his son into service despite his being a child and feels that this entitles the boy to a slightly larger salary, people like Mamata want to hire him but pay less precisely because he is a child. Again, this lays bare one of the aspects of child labour. Throughout the film we notice how experience combines with attitudes, resulting in a particular treatment of Palan. And through Palan, millions of others like him. As in Anjan's explanation of why Palan slept under the stairs:

ANJAN. . . . the previous servants who worked for us used to sleep in that room, you know . . . the sitting room, I mean . . . none of them stayed very long anyway. . . there was one boy . . .] Anyway, that boy, Prasanna, used to work here. But one day he absconded with some things from that room. And since then we've become rather suspicious . . . [trails away into silence].

But it is at the spot which symbolizes Palan's permanent absence, the cremation ground, that we are reminded of history in one of its recent and grimmer moods. Through the Naxalite slogans which cover a wall at the burning ground—'We'll take revenge, Samiran, for your death' and 'We won't forget you, Bipul'—we are reminded of a recent history which has significance for both the relatives and friends who are mourning the young village lad, as well as Anjan and his friends, who are paying their embarrassed last respects. The slogans bring home the grim realities of poverty—scarred lives, and the threats resulting from baulked aspirations. They serve as a hint of one possible common future. This is the India that is possible with such attitudes predominant. A fact that elicits a sense of painful recognition amongst most thinking people in the country today.

Unlike the families in the other two films, Anjan and Mamata have no common stock of memories to recuperate from their life in the manifest now. And in Anjan, there are few aspirations other than those of social advancement. Even his connections to his family are mediated through this. Given that, it is not surprising that his relationships to the world are instrumentalist, hardly the basis for forging a relationship of understanding and care with anyone, or anything. Whereas Mamata is at least able to relate to the world through her powerful feelings of love for her child. We notice this early in the film, when Palan is being introduced by his father:

HARAN. My sister named him Palan. She's the one who raised him, after his mother died.

Mamata looks startled and seems a bit disturbed by the news. She looks down at her son intently for an instant.

MAMATA. I see.

HARAN (*off-screen*). He's my youngest.

Mamata looks at Haran directly again.

It is this ability to connect, mediated through the powerful feelings of maternal love, which saves Mamata from lapsing into Anjan's state of putative uncaring. It also saves her from Anjan's habit of instantly ascribing blame when questioned or brought face to face with the consequences of his actions and attitudes. She is, therefore, considerably more transparent and self-critical. And it is precisely this difference which opens up the yawning gap between them. For Mamata is the one closest to Anjan and thus the nearest target for blame. Nor is there enough sharing between them to try and bridge the distance that, in the end, separates them.

Cut to the interior of the Sens' bedroom. The camera slowly pans right, revealing Anjan and Mamata lying in bed, with a sleeping Pupai between them. It is clear that a strained distance has grown between the couple. Anjan is lying on his back smoking and staring into nothingness. He seems quite oblivious to everyone's presence. Mamata looks at her husband, then turns on her side. Her back is now to him.

This—the film would suggest permanent—estrangement of husband and wife in the sequence, represents the working out of a theme that runs as an undercurrent through all three films. How certain crucially important yet generally elided individuals cast their shadow more in their absence than whilst present. This is true both of their physical as well as their psychological being. Poltu, for instance, needs his oldest sister to be with him, reading him a story as reassurance when he is injured. He also needs her brand of comfort, presumably, since he is so dissatisfied with everyone else's. Similarly, Neeta not only misses her father as an individual, a person, but also for what he represents, an austere academic in a commercially-oriented educational system, a man committed to his own values. Chinu too, represents in her own way, even if within the circumscribed limits of a genteel lower middle-class background, a person who is committed to her own values. The exception to this is *Kharij*, where the psychological dimension has been more or less subordinated to the social. Palan, a desperately poor village child, is attempting to survive—unsuccessfully, as it happens—in the big city. But if Palan has no psychological dimensions, he is a truly stark reminder of the powerful forces that underpin both urban and rural life in this country. Poverty, deprivation and the lack of a future have brought Palan to the city. He and his family, as already mentioned, not only form an impoverished mirror image of Pupai's upwardly mobile one, but, together, the families comprise a composite image of India. This is one reason why Palan's death is linked—via media the slogans painted on the wall in the cremation grounds-to such ominous possibilities as peasant *jacquerie* and insurrectionary movements. And why the feelings that Palan's death gives rise to, especially in Anjan, are those arising from being the focus of social opprobrium. He fears being found legally culpable as much as the thought of being the cause of a child's death, even if through omission rather than commission.

All three people, Chinu, Sasank, and the child Palan do share one important feature. The disappearance of each of the three protagonists brings out sharply how thin the family bonds are. The 'ties that bind' are not as strong as imagined and, indeed, require renewal. Moreover, their disappearance shows how easy it is for a group of people, small or big, to fragment when the pressure falls on the right places. The guilt and resentment generated by being dependent on a daughter of marriageable age, who is—dutifully, of course—sacrificing her own happiness for her family's sake; the problems of living with a reserved and possibly cold academic, whose values are not only somewhat incomprehensible to most of his family, but also seen by them as a major impediment to their social betterment; the discomfort of being held responsible for the death—through negligence—of an underage servant, for a couple of whom only one partner acknowledges the responsibility of succeeding in society; these are some of the fault lines along which these groups fall apart under pressure. This is the facade of family solidarity, a thin crust behind which resentments, frustrations and myriad petty humiliations are seething to break out; all that is required is the appropriate precipitant.

And thus it is that we witness how Chinu's family convert what was initially a soul-searching session into an occasion to flay one another. Minu starts off by attempting to explore the common responsibility they share in setting the trajectory of Chinu's life. As she puts it, 'We've never spared a single thought for Didi until now. We've simply carried on like the selfish creatures that we are.' But bit by bit, as the quarrel gets bitter, she ends up accusing her mother of deliberately refusing to let Chinu marry the man she loved, not merely because she disapproved of him, but in order to keep her income coming.

Mother, however, is not willing to take this cruel comment lying down. It is something everyone has played a part in. The camera has been moving back and forth between the various characters throughout this sequence. Now Mother is centre screen.

MOTHER. And where would you be, if she didn't?
MINU. Yes that's it; say that; speak the truth. That actually we needed her.

Throughout this heated exchanged, Mother has been getting more and more angry at Minu's scathing comments, till, in fury, she accuses Hrishikesh.

The dramatic focus on Mother is reflective of how years of pent-up anger and hurt tend to spill over given the appropriate circumstances. The brief of close-up of her, quivering, and for once, almost out of control—but soon to collapse in tears, is visual confirmation of a tragedy: that fury and anguish concealed over decades have at last been given a vent through which they explode. The sequence ends as it ought, with Mother collapsing in tears of rage and frustration—and Hrishikesh remaining as tongue-tied as ever.

Such psychodrama, however, is not restricted to this family alone. Similar confrontations take place amongst the members of the other two families as well. And in that sense, the estrangement of Anjan and Mamata merely carries the logic of these films to its end. Given what we (do not) know about them, it seems rational that they abruptly discover that love is not enough to keep a couple together.

Nevertheless, all the above notwithstanding, it would be a mistake to imagine that these three films take an entirely bleak view of familial bonds and loyalties. Or that they emphasize the general futility of attempting to triumph against the forces tending to fissiparity, whether these spring from within or are imposed from without. For each of these families, the films suggest, does have the emotional strength to pull together when confronted by adversity. In the face of an overwhelming social stress, these people discover that they can, and indeed must, stand together as a unit. It is ironic, but entirely logical, that it is the absent person who forces this necessity of sticking together on the others of the family. Thus, it is consistent that Chinu's actual reappearance at her home precipitates the crisis, forcing her family to take stock and finally decide to stand by her. The appearance of an individual-a key individual, it goes without saying—in the frame, becomes the occasion for an examination of the social. Chinu's initial confrontation of her family with her presence reminds them acutely of the precarious nature of their lower-middle-class existence. A daughter who can be absent all night, can also, perhaps, even leave one day, and thus deprive the family of its only breadwinner. There is certainly not the slightest indication in the film that Topu, Chinu's brother, will ever manage to find employment. And that, too, is consistent with social reality in a state such as West Bengal, with its tradition of low job creation and high numbers of college-educated unemployed. At the same time, it equally forcefully raises the possibility of severe social censure. For a young woman staying out all night, with no explanation—none is available in the film, in a sense its most powerful ideological declaration—is the subject of gossip as well as severest criticism. Moreover, it reflects badly on her sense of loyalty. At the end of the family confrontation, after Mother slumps in tears, the camera cuts from face to face in a series of close-ups. First to a grim-faced Topu, then to Hrishikesh, who leaves the room silently. The final close-up is of Minu:

> MINU. We'll forget Didi. And any relationships that might have existed with the people in the neighbourhood. After all, we'll have to leave this flat and take a cheaper one. I'll have to give up my studies . . . and take up a job. Then, one night, you'll wait for me in the same way. Stay up all night, inform the police, visit hospitals and what have you, and so on and so forth. But I won't return. Like Didi, I'll . . . (*She bites her lip, then rises and sits on another chair next to the window.*) And Didi, even you only thought of yourself. You didn't think of us, either. I'd thought of you as somehow different, but in the end, you turned out to be as selfish as the rest of us . . .

The rather self-pitying tone notwithstanding, the social and psychological dilemmas of such an existence are thus laid bare. Meanwhile, Chinu gets the unpleasant shock of being at the receiving end of an act of betrayal by her family. Certainly, she is the subject of an act of temporary disloyalty at least; and that too, at a vulnerable moment. As the camera cuts between the various family members, starting with Chinu entering the courtyard and being greeted by a stony-faced family group, we see the hurt, guilt, anguish and realization of betrayal being played out. Chinu's bitter accusation, 'If I'd had an accident you'd have had nothing to say . . .' is entirely appropriate. An accident would add the cachet of further victimhood to this family, thus functioning—in a perverse manner—as an explanatory context. In the event, Chinu has to endure the backlash of their concerns and fears. The camera leaves her isolated in the middle of the courtyard, exposed to the gaze of the neighbours crowding the balconies, with everyone in her family except Topu and her father walking out on her. She walks indoors, to an equally inhospitable welcome.

This is the moment—of partial reckoning—when the landlord, Dwarik Mullick, makes his intervention. He accosts Hrishikesh, accuses Chinu of being disreputable and as Hrishikesh to leave as quickly as possible with his family. In doing so, however, he forces the family to discover the resilience which is also part of this complex set of ties. It is clear that running away in shame would only make Minu's bleak prognostications come true. Acceding to the self-important and sanctimonious Dwarik's demands would mean sacrificing both their oldest daughter as well as their respectability. Indeed, it is in defending Chinu from such moralists that their respectability and survival as a family lies. This is the course that they choose, each in his or her own way. Young and irate, Topu exposes Dwarik for the pompous bully he is. First, he assaults Dwarik physically and frightens him to the point of appealing for help from the onlookers. More importantly, he rejects Dwarik's notions of respectability: 'So what if he's the bloody landlord, he doesn't own us. Respectability, eh? I'll give him respectability. I'll kick him in his respectable teeth, is what I'll do . . .' Hrishikesh remains his tongue-tied self even against this latest assault on his dignity, but he demonstrates his feelings by gently stroking Chinu's head as she bursts into tears. Minu leads her sister away; by now, Mother is doing all in her power to hold back her tears. It is this mutual sustenance which gives these people the strength to start the next day, when the familiar grim rituals of daily survival start afresh. What this might be like is exemplified by the final shot of Mother, seen through the bars of the kitchen window, obscured by smoke and weighed down by the burden of her thoughts.

Similarly, a year's soul-searching leaves Sasank's wife and children with the strength to carry on. The cut here is to a similar monsoon evening, with lightning flashing against an overcast sky—much the same sort of evening as when Sasank disappeared. His family have discovered the worst; that they may well have been wrong about the missing man. The operative word here, of course, is 'may'. We do not know, and never will. But all this discovery has not left them entirely without resources. They have their memories, the capacity to acknowledge that they might have been mistaken in their judgements, and the fortitude to live with their mistakes.

But this is not true of Anjan and Mamata. They simply do not have the emotional wherewithal to endure the intense pressures that devolve upon them consequent to Palan's death. Their relationship, it appears, has secretly foundered while they pursued success and comfort. The death of a child becomes the device which reveals that such success can—at least in the Indian context—literally cause the death of another human being. An indifference to a child's needs, combined with thoughtless disregard for a child's safety, and calm exploitation lie at the root of Palan's sad death. Indeed, a significant part of the tragedy is the fact that it is accidental, even if it was an accident merely biding its time. Even worse, the nature of this success seems especially threadbare since it fails to provide any comfort at a moment of acute need. The couple is found wanting even in a single-minded commitment to success at any cost, since neither can really escape torments of conscience. And if Anjan comes across badly in the film, Mamata, too, has her ghosts to haunt her. She is the one who sets out the interminable tasks which engage a young boy till late at night. Moreover, she is negligent enough not to have considered the attraction of an unventilated kitchen on a bitterly cold night, the only refuge for an otherwise unprotected child. As the film ends, the aridity of their lives has estranged the couple and the guilt, especially that relating to Palan-there-but-for-the-grace-of-God-go-I-Pupai, has driven what seems to be a permanent wedge between them. There would appear to be no real way of remaining immune to such social pressures.

All the three films are explorations—in their own way—of the difficulties inherent in maintaining a sense of autonomy. The protagonists, or, more accurately, Sasank and Chinu, attempt to maintain an individual identity against the grain of the expectations current in their respective milieus. In other words, in the face of middle and lower-middle-class conformity. (It may be equally difficult to maintain it in the face of upper-class conformity, but Sen has no comments to make on that.) The problems inherent in such an enterprise stem not only from the difficulty in raising a dissonant voice against the chorus of routine expectations, nor from the consequences of a dissenting act. They also arise from the fact that the autonomy is very partial at best, and fatally compromised by being dependent on the actions of others. An excellent device for examining the limits and ambiguities of such an existence is provided by Sasank's study. In a sense, the study and the books in it are illustrative of Sasank: they are the concrete source of his erudition and thus part of the foundation of his intellectual—and social—arrogance. They are representative of the world which engages him so considerably—that of the intellect. And at the same time, the study is the haven which permits Sasank to remain so aloof from the world he despises, that of the ordinary 'non-intellectual' concerns of day-to-day life. We see all these facets of his temperament at work during the sequence where he refuses to teach in a 'Tutorial Home' (i.e., a cramming school) newly opened by his friend Arun. Not for him the sort of student who needs guidance through the intricacies of cramming. When reminded that money is useful and prices keep going up, Sasank's response is quite characteristic of his attitude. 'I don't know anyhing about that. That's not something that I get involved in. In any case, these people never tell me anything.' His wife's protestations to the contrary are of little consequence.

Several times in the film, the camera underlines the importance of this room by panning over the shelves of books. On one of the few occasions when Sasank seems genuinely relaxed and happy, he is in the library; as when Neeta catches him at his desk, reading late into the night. They share a joke about the one-handed clock that he retains against all reason. These are not objects that his family, including his beloved daughter Neeta, have much to do with. Nor does Sasank want them even dusted. 'Don't you touch anything of mine,' he tells his wife in public. 'I don't care if this room turns into a rubbish dump.' All because he has been unable to locate certain journals! Nor are Sasank's family unaware of the significance (especially as *mementoes mori?*) of these books. It is, therefore, entirely appropriate that the sequence in which he is told that he has been accused of plagiarism takes place in the study. It is the consciousness that Sasank's absence is possibly immutable, that has made his family agree to part with the books. In the final sequence, we are back where we started—in the monsoons. It is a year since Sasank disappeared—the books have by now been donated to a library—and his family are taking stock. After a succession of shots of a sky in the throes of a wild monsoon storm, the camera pans over the faces of Sasank's disconsolate family members, sitting on the floor of a dimly-lit study, leaning against the shelves. They are empty. Sasank's absence is now truly palpable. His identification with his books now seems complete, to his family as much as to us.

All this having been said, however, this image of Sasank turns out to be curiously riven by fault lines. Any number of ambiguities lurk under the surface, which are at variance with the image of the dedicated and uncompromising academic. One of the most interesting things about the collection of books, with which Sasank is so identified, is that they are not his collection at all. The collection has come to Sasank through inheritance, having been in the main put together by his late father, as he tells Aparna. Even the indexing was done by his father. Sasank's contribution, in the main, seems to consist of maintaining a sort of proprietary guardianship of his library whilst keeping his 'non-intellectual' family away from the books. And just as this image of the bibliophile is undercut by the reality of the original ownership, so is the image of the aloof academic. The calm facade cracks when he learns that he has been accused of plagiarism as well as incompetence. A 'controversial' essay by him has been fiercely attacked, the writer accusing Sasank, among other things, of being incapable of dealing with the subject. For the first time, Sasank's cool exterior cracks. But worst of all, this is precisely the moment when his beloved library lets him down as well. He takes tremendous umbrage at this; he is certainly not mollified by Aparna's suggestion that he should have been more careful in his original article. But his attempts to counter the accusation prove to be in vain. He is unable to locate the journals which would help him to refute the charge of plagiarism and carelessness. The frantic searching only leads to increased exasperation and leaves him further agitated. The all-important journals are simply not to be found. The image of Sasank, the calm, aloof and uncompromising intellectual, suddenly fractures and for a moment, the picture of a different Sasank emerges: one whose self-control, and intellectual integrity are under question. More, it becomes evident that Sasank's self-sufficiency is, in part at least based on the work of others. His precious books were mostly acquired by his father; his daughter's income contributes to his financial wellbeing; the house he lives in was inherited from his father; and last, if he can afford to remain uninvolved in the business of running a household, it is mainly because his wife has taken over the responsibility of dealing with the humdrum chores of everyday life.

Similarly, Chinu, too, has gained an independence which is to a degree more imagined than real. Though it needs to be emphasized that this autonomy is by no means illusory, either; merely circumscribed. The fact that she returns but does not offer any explanation for why she stayed out suggests that her family accept, however grudgingly, this independence. Her autonomy is underscored by the fact that several of the other female characters see her actions as worthy of emulation. Her younger sister Minu and the girl Lily, to name two. Not surprisingly, both of them have firm opinions on the question of a woman leading an autonomous existence. There are other hints that she is cutting across the grain as far as social expectations are concerned. For instance, that she has no truck with any relative, a matter of some significance in a country where family ties are of paramount importance. And, of course, there is the fact that she is the economic mainstay of her family. Nevertheless, the very fact that she is the sole breadwinner for a large family places constraints on her field of actions. Moreover, that she has accepted this role of her volition, as her duty, only goes to make her autonomy even more contingent. Her ability to break free is circumscribed by her family's dependence on her continuing presence. This remains true even in those circumstances which concern her future happiness, as in the case of her then possible marriage to Somnath. He, of course, is killed, thereby terminating all possibilities. But by then, the chances of this marriage taking place had been rendered nearly non-existent. Not merely because of her mother's disapproval, but also through her acceptance of her mother's right to choose. If Mother withheld approval, Chinu too refused to press the issue. At the same time, it remains true that Chinu is able to be absent—Monday to Friday, nine to five— because Mother and the rest remain home. Here, it is redundant that she needs to be absent as much as they are prevented from leaving. What is important is that recognized and accepts this dynamic and following on from that, does the best she can to discharge the resulting responsibilities.

Anjan, on the other hand, can hardly be accused of being at cross-purposes to the standard expectations of the society he belongs to. He remains in a very real sense a paradigm case of the upwardly aspiring—if not yet fully mobile—young man. If he is marooned finally in this enterprise, as in any others to do with mutuality, it is an entirely consistent end for someone who seems to consider a rather self-centred, to say nothing of selfish, philosophy the appropriate means for advancing in the world. He has an instrumentalist attitude regarding other people, in that they are either implements or impediments to his advancement. None of this to suggest that Anjan is in any sense a bad person. He is, in fact, a perfectly decent sort. It is just that this somewhat solipsistic notion limits his perceptions regarding everyone other than his own family. It also leaves him unable to acknowledge that he has any liability—other than that of doing the best he can—for the consequences of his actions. Virtually every time his actions are called to question, no matter how petty the circumstance, he tries to fob off the burden on to someone else. He can only envision consequences in terms of good or ill for himself, based on the narrowest of criteria. Unfortunately, the death of young Palan signifies much more than mere social opprobrium for his master. Ultimately, Anjan is forced to confront this fact through a series of incidents, culminating in Sreela's grandfather's enquiry whether 'they' had caused him any problems at the cremation grounds. By now his innate decency has asserted itself and he is very uncomfortable. But it is too little and far too late. By now he has even been estranged from his wife.

Chinu and Sasank's absence forces some degree of reconsideration of their lives, and therefore their pasts, upon their respective families. The resulting confrontations may even have brought about some changes in their perceptions of one another. In contrast, Anjan's life is rocked by the absence of another person. The circumstances that brought this about were ones that he had been partly instrumental in creating. He is, of course, quite indifferent to the past. In addition, his personal philosophy, such as it is, is ill-designed for anything other than rationalizing his smug pursuit of self-betterment. When this itself comes under question, he has nothing left to fall back upon or bridge the gaps that have opened up between him and his wife, Mamata. He is thus left both isolated as well as stranded. Sasank, on the other hand, seems well pleased with his lot and revels in the role of rectitudinous and uncompromising academic. Yet his image, too, turns out to be misleading in several crucial areas. Sasank shows as little inclination to confront these areas as, say, Anjan. He simply vanishes one day. (Why? The answer, like the one to why Chinu suddenly decides to stay out one night, is one of those intriguing 'absences') It is only Chinu who has accepted—whether happily or grudgingly—that there are constraints on her life and still done her best by everyone. It is appropriate that she should return home with her dignity intact, and that she should ultimately have her family's support. Without having to explain where she had been all night, or why.

Somnath Zutshi, 1999

---

1 John W. Hood, *Chasing The Truth: The Films of Mrinal Sen* (Calcutta: Seagull Books, 1993), p. 107.

2 Mrinal Sen, 'Rambling Thoughts', *Social Scientist* 25(3–4) (March–April 1997).

3 In other words, 'Every Day'. For reasons unknown, *Ekdin Pratidin* was translated as *And Quiet Flows the Dawn*. Aside from the rather unfortunate resonance of Russian revolutionary novels, the translation—apart from being simply wrong—is entirely misleading. *Ekdin Pratidin* is not only best—and most legitimately—rendered as 'One Day/Everyday/Each Day', there is not a bit of quietude about this intense film. Moreover, dawn has virtually nothing to do with the main body of the film. Nor does it flow quietly, since Chinu arrives home a little before dawn, following which the altercation etc. takes place.

...And Quiet Rolls the Dawn

Ekdin Pratidin (1979)

Translated from the Bengali
Based on a Story by Amalendu Chakraborty

Credits

Produced, directed, scripted by	Mrinal Sen
Photography	K. K. Mahajan
Music	B. V. Karanth
Art design	Suresh Chandra
Editing	Gangadhar Naskar

Cast

Artistes	*Characters*
Satya Banerjee	Hrishikesh
Geeta Sen	Mother
Mamata Shankar	Chinu
Sreela Majumder	Minu
Umanath Bhattacharya	Dwarik Mullick
Arun Mukherjee	Shyamal
and others	

35 mm/normal screen 1.1.33/95 min/Eastmancolor

The film starts with a list of acknowledgements against a white screen.

Long shot of a very narrow lane, dark and dank, that almost looks like a tunnel from this perspective. The buildings on both sides are covered with moss and damp patches. The plaster is peeling off from most walls. By the side of the lane runs an open drain. The entire atmosphere reeks of neglect and decay. At the far end, where the lane joins the road, the light is momentarily obscured. A rickshaw appears at the mouth of the lane, accompanied by the sound of bells. The rickshaw moves slowly towards the camera. As it completes about one-third of the distance, the title of the film, EKDIN PRATIDIN, appears. The rickshaw keeps moving closer to the camera; about two-thirds of the way, the title EKDIN PRATIDIN appears again. The rickshaw approaches and then passes the camera, eventually moving out of the frame. The lane is empty once again.

Cut to close-up of a pair of hands vigorously working the handle of a hand pump, while a boy of eleven or twelve drinks water.

Cut to a group of ten or twelve boys noisily playing football.

Cut to close-up of an adult blowing on a whistle; he is obviously officiating as the referee.

Cut to boys playing football. This time the camera follows them around, until the entire road is revealed in long shot, whilst the children keep playing. At a distance, the rickshaw can now be seen approaching. It is followed by another group of boys, much the same age as the young footballers. The second group is, however, led by an older boy. As this group approaches the football players, they become silent. The rickshaw moves out of the frame. The group moves on.

Cut to the front door of a house. A young man in his early twenties steps out. He is dressed in a sleeveless vest and pyjamas, and is smoking. He sees the approaching group and quickly walks up to them.

AMAL. My God! How did that happen?

Cut to mid-shot of a little boy surrounded by others, whose faces cannot be seen. The boy is bleeding from a gash over his right eyebrow. The young man turns the boy's face to examine the wound.

OLDER BOY. He fell while playing in the park.

AMAL. Well, what did you bring him here for? (*To little boy*) Let's get you to the doctor.

POLTU. No! I won't go to the doctor. He'll give me an injection. I shan't go, I shan't.

Cut to lane. A young woman peeks out from a doorway, takes one look and comes running.

MINU. Oh Lord! What've you gone and done now?

The little boy holds her tight.

POLTU. Mejdi . . . !

Cut to a close-up of Amal and Minu, seen from the back.

Cut to Dulal looking angrily over the counter of the pharmacy.

DULAL. Hey . . . hey, what's going on here? Clear off, you lot. Stop crowding about here . . . go on . . .

Cut to Dulal moving round the counter. As the camera follows him, it reveals a horde of children crowding round the counter. Dulal starts shooing them away, joined by Amal.

AMAL. Go on, push off. What on earth d'you lot think you're doing? Go on, now.

DULAL. Go on, I said, run along. They've turned it into a fish market!

Cut to mid-shot of a recumbent Poltu. The doctor bandages his head, whilst helping him sit up. Poltu is making an anguished face.

DOCTOR. There now, sit up for a bit. Everything's going to be all right. These things happen sometimes. Does it hurt much?

POLTU. Yes.

DOCTOR. Just one more minute. One does get hurt a little whilst playing. There's a smart boy. Good lad.

Cut to an anxious-looking Amal and Minu. Amal turns towards Minu.

AMAL. He's had three stitches put in.

Cut to the doctor in close-up, still bandaging Poltu's head.

DOCTOR. Dulal . . . ?

DULAL. Sir . . . ?

DOCTOR. There's a big crowd outside.

DULAL. There's no one there. I've sent them all away.

Cut to Amal and Minu. Amal turns and leaves. As he walks away, Hrishikesh can be seen in mid-shot. Minu turns and walks out of the door as well, nodding to her father as she passes him.

MINU. Let's go.

Cut to the waiting room. Minu and Hrishikesh are seen in mid-shot, standing face to face.

MINU. Why don't you go home, Baba?

HRISHIKESH. Why?

MINU. Things have settled down now. It'll be over in a few minutes and then I'll bring him home . . .

The camera pans right to show Jhunu in high angle shot, in mid-close-up. Amal can be seen sitting in the background.

MINU. Jhunu, you go home with Baba.

HRISHIKESH. But d'you think you'll be able to manage on your own?

Cut back to the examining room; Poltu and the doctor can be seen in mid-close-up. The doctor dresses Poltu's injury, then helps him stand up. Poltu stands up in a very gingerly sort of fashion, making grimaces of pain all the while.

DOCTOR. There's no great harm done. Little boys are meant to crack their heads, aren't they . . . Next time, climb a tree; that'll really teach you to sleep at home all day. Can you get down? Easy now, slowly, slowly. Dulal . . .

Cut. The credit titles start rolling. The loud ticking of a clock can be heard, followed by music.

Cut, as the credits finish rolling, to an extreme low angle shot of the parapet of a terrace. The camera slowly zooms back, to reveal an ancient, dilapidated, pillared building. A sari is hanging from an upper balcony. The camera slowly tilts down to ground level.

Cut to mid-shot of a barebodied man in a dhoti. He crosses the courtyard from screen right. The camera pans left, following him as he leaves the frame, before coming to rest on a middle-aged woman. She is grey-haired and rather tired looking.

Cut to close-up of woman, as she fills a bucket with water from a reservoir.

Cut to mid-long shot of woman seen from within two columns, as she carries the bucket inside. The camera pans to follow her, as she takes the water bucket in. As she reaches the door of her flat, the camera pans sharply to the right, to show Minu preparing Poltu's medication.

> MOTHER. Have you given him his medicine, dear?
> MINU. Yes, I'll give him one more tablet in a minute.

The camera pans further right, as Minu rises with a glass of water and sits on the bed next to Poltu.

> POLTU. Mejdi, when'll Didi get home?
> MINU. Open your mouth.
> POLTU. But I've just had one!
> MINU. Just open your mouth. Wider . . . now, put the book down and close your eyes. You'll soon fall asleep.
> POLTU. Mejdi . . . ?
> MINU. What is it?
> POLTU. When will Didi return?
> MINU. She'll return . . . she'll return.

Minu rises and walks to Jhunu, who is busy studying at her desk. She puts the magazine down, as well as the tumbler. She takes a book from the pile on the table and uses it to cover the glass.

> POLTU. But when . . . ?
> MINU. She won't return then. Satisfied?

Cut to Mother, who is sitting on the floor, kneading dough.

> MOTHER. What rubbish you can talk sometimes! Anyway, it's long past evening. Whatever can she be up to?

Mother looks over her shoulder towards Minu.

Cut to Minu. She walks behind the bed.

MINU. She's hardly expected to clock in every day, Ma.

Minu picks up a rolled-up mattress and pillows and walks in front of the bed.

MINU. Ma, I'm making the beds.

Cut to mid-close-up of Mother. It can now be seen that she is in a separate room, which is the kitchen, where she is making the dough. It is a small, dark room, with peeling walls.

MOTHER. But why? It's ever so early. What time is it, Jhunu?

Cut to Minu, who is spreading the mattress on the floor.

JHUNU. It's twenty past seven; but our clock is five minutes slow.
MINU. I might as well make the beds. If Poltu falls asleep, it'll be a job waking him up and getting him to sleep on the floor.

Cut to Mother. Minu can be seen in the next room, sitting on the floor.

MOTHER. No, leave him where he is. The way you people sleep, sprawling all over the place, someone might hit him on the head again. He'd better sleep away from you people.
MINU. Will Baba sleep on the floor, then?
MOTHER. He might as well. I'll sleep next to Poltu.

Cut to Poltu in mid-close-up, lying in bed with his head bandaged.

POLTU. No you won't. Didi'll sleep next to me. She'll read me a story.
MINU. Now stop making a fuss. She'll get home dog tired from office and she has to start reading him stories! He's acting as if he's done everyone a great favour by breaking his head.

JHUNU. You're right. (*To Poltu*) Who d'you think you are?

POLTU. Stop talking rubbish! D'you know I've had three stitches put in?

MINU. Oh dear, oh dear! Three stitches, eh. (*To Jhunu*) What are we going to do, Jhunu?

POLTU. Ma, look what Mejdi's doing.

MOTHER. Now stop teasing him, you two.

Minu comes up to Poltu, and sits next to the bed.

POLTU. Why, didn't Amalda tell you about my three stitches?

MINU. Didn't the doctor give your Amalda a good ticking off?

POLTU. That's a rotten doctor.

MINU. That's a lovely doctor.

POLTU. Rotten.

MINU. Lovely.

POLTU. Rotten!

MINU. Lovely!

POLTU. Rotten, rotten!!

MINU. Lovely, lovely!!

POLTU. Rotten, rotten, rotten!!!

MINU. Lovely, lovely, lovely!!!

Minu fondly tweaks Poltu's nose. He cries out in pain. Minu looks rather embarrassed at her excessive affection.

Cut to an anxious Mother who looks at them fearfully.

MOTHER. What happened?

Cut. The camera tracks through the ground level of the house, moving through a forest of columns.

Cut to mid-close-up of Hrishikesh, standing in the courtyard, looking very anxious.

Cuts to different parts of the house, showing various occupants busy with their own lives. In the background can be heard the voice of the narrator.

> NARRATOR. The year 1857 . . . The year of the Indian Mutiny. The year in which this house was built by Babu Nabin Chandra Mullick. And since then, from the East India Company, via Queen Victoria, onto the CMDA, from the division of Bengal to the partition of Bengal, the narrative of the city of Calcutta has been replete with meetings, processions, riots, bloodshed, famines and the occasional war. But despite all this, Calcutta still survives. As does the house on Nabin Chandra Lane, built by Babu Nabin Chandra Mullick.

(Flashback begins.)

Cut to an extreme low angle shot of the facade of the house. The camera slowly tilts down to the ground level, showing Hrishikesh bathing in the courtyard. He is pouring water on himself from a bucket.

> NARRATOR. The present owner is Mr Dwarik Mullick. He lives on the third floor. The remaining sixteen rooms house eleven families. The three rooms on the ground floor are inhabited by Hrishikesh Sengupta. He had come here twenty-three years ago, with his wife and a two-year-old daughter. The family has since increased to seven. Hrishikeshbabu is now retired. His pension is sufficient to pay the rent and for a few sundries.

Cut to low angle shot of the stairway, seen through an arch. Dwarik appears at the top of the stairs, comes down to the courtyard and stands on the porch. He looks at Hrishikesh with a sour expression on his face, then walks across to him.

DWARIK. Just take it easy, Hrishikeshbabu; how much water d'you intend to use? There're other people living in the house after all . . . As if all the bloody responsibilities are mine . . . you know what the Corporation's like.

Hrishikesh looks rather stricken at this telling off. Dwarik leaves; the camera follows Dwarik, who glances backwards occasionally as he goes.

NARRATOR. Dwarik Mullick. The landlord. He certainly cannot be accused of being overfond of his tenants. The wretched creatures block his rooms for decades on end. The price of everything from rice to medicine goes up, but their rents remain the same. Any attempt to increase the rent causes a hundred legal problems. His forefathers used to spend their time ruling their subjects and racing pigeons. His blood retains some traces of its previous aristocratic hauteur.

Dwarik steps out through the front door and slowly walks down the lane. A man walks towards Dwarik, going in the opposite direction. The man walks past Dwarik, then squats down on the side of the road next to the open drain, and starts to urinate.

Cut to close-up of Dwarik, with a look of utter exasperation on his face, watching the man. The man looks up at Dwarik, who is looming over him, grins sheepishly, then turns away again. He finishes and stands up to leave.

DWARIK. Just a minute. What was that?

The man looks at Dwarik in speechless amazement.

Cut to Poltu, who appears at the front door. He is driving a metal hoop with a stick. His head is unbandaged. Poltu has obviously seen the little episode, and enjoyed it. He chuckles.

Cut to Dwarik and the man.

DWARIK. Yes, that.

MAN. Sorry.

The man grins and hurries away. Dwarik makes a disgusted face and walks on. Poltu drives his metal hoop in the opposite direction. The lane becomes empty once again.

(Flashback ends.)

Cut to Poltu lying on the bed. He turns in a restless manner. In the background can be heard the chant of pallbearers passing by—'Bolo Hari, Hari Bol'. The camera rapidly tracks rightwards to mid-close-up of Jhunu at her desk. She rises on hearing the chanting and rushes to screen left. Camera tracks left, back to Poltu who completes his turn to his right side.

Cut; Jhunu rushes to a window; Hrishikesh is already gazing out of it.

Cut to Minu in mid-close-up. She also hurries to another window to look.

Cut back to Jhunu and Hrishikesh.

JHUNU. Who was it, Baba?

HRISHI. Who knows. Come on.

Jhunu and Hrishikesh walk back. Mother can be seen in the background squatting on the floor, washing the dishes. Jhunu carries on past her mother, but Hrishikesh stops next to her.

HRISHI. You know, Chinu's not returned home yet.

MOTHER. I just hope that she's alright . . . (*As she gets up*) I can't even think anymore.

Hrishikesh walks away. Mother finishes washing the dishes and takes them inside. The camera follows her through a labyrinth of corridors and rooms, until she reaches Minu's room. Close-up of

Minu at her table, studying. Mother comes and stands next to her.
Minu is slapping at mosquitoes.

MOTHER. Minu, your sister isn't back as yet.

MINU. I know.

MOTHER. Well, if you know, do something about it.

MINU. Do what?

MOTHER. That's true enough, I suppose. What can you do . . .
Why don't you spray some 'Flit'?

Mother leaves Minu's room.

Cut to Hrishikesh entering the bedroom, drying his face with a
towel. He hangs the towel on the door and crosses the room, screen
right. The camera pans further right, showing Jhunu at her desk.

MOTHER. Jhunu, what's the time, dear?

JHUNU. It's six past eight. But our clock's five minutes' slow.

Cut to Minu, moving past the window. She passes her mother, who
is seen to be cooking.

MINU. Let's wait a while longer.

MOTHER. Do whatever you think's best . . . I . . . I . . . what can
I say?

Cut to Minu, removing a handspray from a shelf. She pauses in
front of the kitchen door. Hrishikesh can be seen in the background, behind Minu.

MINU. Look, Ma, you don't go out anywhere, you've no idea
what the roads are like. Things are in such a bad shape that
an hour or so's delay isn't any cause for worry.

HRISHIKESH. It's not a question of a half hour or an hour's delay,
is it? The point is that Chinu's never home later than half-
past-six.

MINU. Well, she is today, isn't she.

Minu leaves the room.

13

(Flashback begins.)

Cut to a long shot of a Calcutta street in the daytime. The pavement is screen right; about midground is a bus stop. A bus comes to a halt at the bus stop.

Cut to the interior of the jampacked bus. Chinu shoves her way inside, and finally finds a seat beside some other women. A number of people can be seen hanging on for dear life, near the door. The bus moves; cut to mid-close-up of Chinu, who looks over her shoulder.

Cut to street flashing by. As we see the street, the voice of the narrator can be heard off screen.

> NARRATOR. That two-year-old child of twenty-three years ago, now shoves her way through crowds in order to get on a bus like anyone else, works nine to five in an office, and acts as the meal ticket for a family of seven. She provides the school fees for her younger brother and sister, the college expenses for her other sister, to say nothing of dole money for her generally unemployed brother.

(Flashback ends.)

Cut to Minu standing in front of the dressing table. She cleans her face and then examines herself in the mirror, before sitting down at her desk. She looks through a small diary, notes down a telephone number and gets up.

Cut to bedroom. Poltu is lying down, with Hrishikesh sitting on a chair near the head of the bed. Through the open door, Mother can be seen in the kitchen. Minu enters through door and leaves screen left. Mother enters behind her with a brass cup containing milk, which she hands over to Hrishikesh.

MOTHER. Could you hold this for a moment?

Mother sits on the bed next to the sleeping Poltu, and wakes her son.

MOTHER. Poltu, wake up darling, and drink your milk . . . Come on love, wake up; you shouldn't sleep on an empty stomach. Get up, dear.

She takes the brass cup from Hrishikesh.

MOTHER. Hold the plate.

Makes Poltu drink the milk.

HRISHIKESH. It's nine o'clock. She's not back yet. She isn't visiting a friend, is she?

MOTHER. Well, she could at least let us know.

Cut to Minu, who is putting some change into her purse. She turns to look at her mother.

MINU. Why?

MOTHER. What on earth d'you mean, why? Oughtn't she to tell us that she's going to be late?

MINU. You've sent your daughter out to work, Ma. You can't have everything, you know . . . Anyway, I'm just going to the chemists.

MOTHER. Why to the chemists?

MINU. I'll ring Didi's office from there.

HRISHIKESH. Her office? This late at night?

Minu leaves without responding. Hrishikesh gets up with a worried expression on his face and follows her to the door.

Cut to high angle shot of Calcutta at night. Streams of cars can be seen moving in the dimly lit streets.

Cut to man at pharmacy, standing next to the door. Minu appears at the door, hesitates and then enters.

MINU. Could I make a telephone call, please?

DULAL. Yes, go ahead.

Minu starts phoning.

Cut to Dwarik, who is seen sitting in a chair reading a paper. He looks at Minu once, then goes back to his paper.

Cut to close-up of Minu as she anxiously waits to speak. She puts the phone down in disappointment, then tries again.

Cut to a shot of the interior of the pharmacy. Minu can be seen in the foreground, at the phone. Dulal is behind the counter, talking to a customer. The doctor enters from the door at the rear of the shop.

DOCTOR. Dulal, I'm leaving now. Hand me my bag, will you … If Dr Roy rings, tell him that I'll phone him tomorrow. And tell any patients that turn up to come tomorrow morning.

DULAL. Yes, all right then.

The doctor walks across to stand next to Minu.

DOCTOR. How's your brother?

MINU. Okay.

DOCTOR. He's not complaining of pain any longer, is he?

MINU. No.

DOCTOR. If he does, give him a Crocin. Have you got some at home?

MINU. Yes.

DOCTOR. In case you don't, Dulal will give you some. And let me know if there's any change in his condition.

The doctor leaves, moving out of frame screen right. Minu puts the phone down with a thoughtful expression on her face, then dials again.

Cut to the customer at the till.

Cut to Dwarik, still reading his paper.

Cut to over-the-shoulder shot of Minu and Dulal. Minu puts the phone down.

> DULAL. Aren't you going to speak?
> MINU. I keep getting a 'no-reply' tone.
> DULAL. A 'no-reply' tone? Here, let me see that number. Double two? That's a business district number.
> MINU. Yes, it's Didi's office.
> DULAL. Didi's office?

Dulal looks at his watch.

Cut to Dwarik, who also looks at his watch.

> DULAL (*off-screen*). This late?
> CUSTOMER. It's nine-five.

Cut to Minu in mid-close-up.

> MINU. She's doing overtime, you know. I think she must've left . . . I might as well go myself.

Cut to customer in mid-close-up as Minu walks past. Dwarik looks at Minu as she leaves the chemist's shop.

Cut to mid-shot of Hrishikesh, seen through the arches on the ground floor of the building. It is quite dark by now. The camera follows Hrishikesh as he climbs a flight of stairs and enters his bedroom. He is looking weary with anxiety. The camera pans to show the interior of the bedroom through the bars of a window. Mother can be seen on the far side of the bedroom, looking rather tired and forlorn. She is sitting next to a curtained window. Hrishikesh enters and sits on the bed with his back to the camera.

17

Cut to mid-close-up of Mother, in a state of virtual exhaustion, then cut back to Hrishikesh, sitting on the bed. Poltu can be seen lying behind him.

HRISHIKESH. Perhaps she's gone to Srirampur, to visit your sister.

MOTHER. She'll never visit a relative.

Cut to a high angle shot of Jhunu and Poltu sleeping on the bed.

HRISHIKESH. Now Jhunu's fallen asleep as well. Jhunu . . . Jhunu!

JHUNU. I'm not asleep.

MOTHER. You will be in a minute, though. Why don't you go and have your dinner?

JHUNU. I'm just going . . .

MOTHER. Never mind this just going business. Go and eat, it's quite late. And put your father's dinner out as well; I'm feeling very tired. I can't manage any more . . . Well? Jhunu . . . Jhunu!

JHUNU. What is it?

MOTHER. Go and eat your dinner. Go and wash your face, then eat.

Jhunu sits up on the bed, her back to the camera.

JHUNU. Why don't you put the dinner out?

MOTHER. You mean you can't help yourself one day? What d'you take me for?

Camera zooms very slightly.

JHUNU. Well, you're just sitting there!

Cut. Jhunu crosses camera in extreme close-up and leaves frame screen right. Mother is seen in mid-close-up. She looks very angry.

MOTHER. I'm just sitting, am I? Perhaps it's because I can barely manage to stand.

Cut. Minu appears at the bedroom door. Jhunu crosses her and then stops.

MINU. What's going on here?

JHUNU. Just look at Ma, Mejdi. She's snapping my head off for no reason at all.

MINU. Yes, so I've noticed all evening.

Cut to Mother in mid-close-up. She rises from her chair in fury, dabbing at her face with her sari.

MOTHER. What've you noticed, eh? What?

Cut to mid-close-up of Hrishikesh. He looks quite distraught at all this squabbling.

HRISHIKESH. Stop it, you people.

Cut to Minu. She looks at her parents in a disgusted manner and then leaves.

Cut to Hrishikesh in close-up. He rises and walks off after Minu. The camera pans to follow him. An off-screen voice can be heard, calling after Minu.

Cut to the arches on the ground floor. An elderly, bespectacled and grey-haired woman can be seen, hobbling across with the help of a stick. She is wearing the traditional white sari of the Bengali widow.

OLD LADY. Minu . . . Minu, what's wrong, dear?

MINU (*off-screen*). Were you saying something, grandma?

OLD LADY. You went somewhere in a rush and came back in an equal rush. Whatever's going on?

MINU (*off-screen*). Oh, I'd just gone to the chemists.

OLD LADY. Your brother's alright, isn't he?

MINU. Yes grandma, he's asleep.

OLD LADY. Oh, good.

The old lady nods and leaves.

Cut to Minu and Hrishikesh in mid-shot, standing in the court-yard in the semi-darkness.

MINU (*to her father*). Come.

Minu walks away rapidly. The camera follows her, showing Hrishikesh walking behind her. Minu stops at the door of her parent's bedroom. Mother can be seen on the far side of the room, standing beside the bed. Hrishikesh comes to the door from screen left.

MINU. The office's shut. There's no one there.

MOTHER. I wish Topu were here now.

MINU. Fat lot of good he'll do. We'll have to wait for ever if we decide to wait for him. In any case, when does he ever get home before midnight?

MOTHER. He returned in the early hours of the morning, bolted some thing down by afternoon and left again. Apparently, he had some urgent business somewhere! God only knows what he's up to—he certainly never tells us anything.

(Flashback begins.)

Cut to the ground floor, porch. It is daytime. Topu is standing on the porch.

TOPU. Ma, where's the what's-it-called gone? You know, the thingamajig that used to be here.

Topu is seen through the archways, frantically searching for something.

MOTHER. What on earth d'you mean, a what's-it-called? Why don't you say what you're looking for?

TOPU. Oh, you know—a hammer. Didn't we used to have a hammer?

MOTHER. A hammer?

TOPU. That's right.

MOTHER. Now where would you find a hammer in this house?

TOPU. You know what I mean. The thing you use on the coal
and so on . . . I don't understand what you people're up to.
One can't find anything when one needs it. And the whole
place is full of unnecessary and rubbishy stuff . . . I do wish
you lot would stop putting things in order . . .

He suddenly seems to discover what he requires. It is a pestle,
which Topu uses to hammer some loose nails in his sandals.

TOPU. . . . There, the pestle. That'll do.

Cut to Mother in mid-long shot. She is washing clothes at one
corner of the courtyard, but has seen Topu pouncing upon the pestle. She starts walking towards him.

MOTHER. What're you doing with that pestle?

TOPU. Grinding spices!

By now Mother has come up to Topu and tries to take the pestle
away from him.

MOTHER. That's not funny, Topu. You're hammering your sandals
with that pestle. Come on, hand it over . . . come on.

TOPU. It's this nail . . . look, this one here.

MOTHER. Come on, love. You can't want to repair that filthy san-
dal with this . . . I'll give you something else. You give that
pestle back now . . . Oh dear Lord, now he's hammering the
soles. Who knows how filthy they are.

TOPU. And what about the fact that the nails're boring holes in
my feet? All you've got to do is to wash the damned thing
in soap and water, anyway.

MOTHER. No, no . . . no, thank you. I don't want it any more.
Don't you dare put it back there. You throw that pestle away,
you hear me. Ughh . . . filthy creature . . . ughhh . . .

(Flashback ends.)

Cut to high angle shot of a dark Calcutta street. Car headlights are winding by.

Cut to the distant lights of an approaching tramcar, seen in the darkness.

Cut to the interior of the tramcar. Shyamal is seen sitting next to a window. The tramcar comes to a stop and Shyamal gets up. The camera pans slightly to the right, to focus on Hrishikesh waiting at the stop. Shyamal alights from the tramcar and stops next to Hrishikesh.

> SHYAMAL. Why hello, Hrishikeshbabu. What're you doing here at this hour?
>
> HRISHIKESH. Er . . . nothing . . . just like that, you know.
>
> SHYAMAL. You do realize that this is the last tram, don't you?

Shyamal walks away. The tram continues on its way.

Cut to close-up of Hrishikesh, looking at the receding tramcar. The sound of the tramcar slowly fades away; Hrishikesh looks dejected and lost.

Cut to Mother peeking through the front door. She gazes from screen right to left as we hear a rickshaw passing by off-screen. Shyamal comes up to the door and then stops.

> SHYAMAL. Hello! You here?
>
> MOTHER. Oh, just like that.
>
> SHYAMAL. I saw Hrishikeshbabu at the tram stop.
>
> MOTHER. Oh! By the way, did you hear of any trouble anywhere?
>
> SHYAMAL. Trouble? Why, no. But why d'you ask?
>
> MOTHER. No reason, really. Just that there's always some trouble or the other brewing on the roads these days, isn't there?

Shyamal looks at her rather quizzically, then walks away.

Cut to Mother, still looking anxiously through the door.

Cut to Mother with her back to the camera. Minu appears from screen left and joins her at the door.

MOTHER. How deserted the entire neighbourhood's looking.

MINU. What was Shyamalda saying?

MOTHER. That he saw your father on the road.

MINU. How long's Father going to wait on the road by himself? And that, too, at this odd hour?

Cut to Dwarik in close-up, at the door.

DWARIK. Minu, hasn't Hrishikeshbabu returned yet? . . . Well, you'd better lock the front door, then.

Dwarik looks at them once again and leaves.

Cut to Minu and Mother, still looking anxiously at the road.

MINU. There's Baba.

Hrishikesh appears at the doorway, looks at the two women and slowly nods his head. The women look at one another.

HRISHIKESH. Come on.

Minu and Mother leave. The camera slowly zooms into a close-up of Hrishikesh, who looks through the doorway once and then slowly walks off. Fade to black.

Cut to low angle shot of the facade of the building. It is night. The top two floors are lit.

Cut to the balcony, where Shyamal can be seen leaning against the railing, smoking thoughtfully, looking deeply preoccupied; in the background, the last radio bulletin can be heard off-screen.

Cut to the interior of a room. A woman can be seen at the far end, preparing *paan*. A man with his back to the camera is seen in extreme close-up.

NAREN. I guessed that something was wrong there and then. I notice that Hrishikeshda's returned.

WIFE . Well, he's her father, after all. For all you know, he's gone back to the road once again.

NAREN. But where can the girl have gone? She's not like most other women of her age, is she?

WIFE. I just hope that she hasn't been involved in an accident, or anything like that. You know, the sort of thing that's always taking place in Calcutta.

NAREN. Yes, quite. Remember the bus that overturned opposite the Birla Planetarium?

WIFE. Don't I just. That Pintu, he'd only been married a few months. My God! If something like that's happened, what's going to become of this family?

Abrupt cut to close-up of a sour-faced old man, lying in bed.

GIRIN. To perdition, I tell you; that entire family'll go to perdition. I'm sure that girl's eloped with someone. That's it, she's eloped.

Cut to a teenager studying at a desk. She is sitting at the opposite end of the room. The girl looks at the old man sarcastically as he sits up in bed after passing his comments. His wife, a middle-aged woman, can be seen in the background putting a pillow slip on a pillow.

LILY. What rubbish!

GIRIN. What was that? What did you say?

LILY. Really, Granddad, don't you know Auntie Chinu? Haven't you seen her from when she was about this high? Is she the sort to elope?

GIRIN'S WIFE. You shut your mouth, young lady. Always sticking her nose where it's not wanted.

LILY. You're exactly like him you know, Grandma.

GIRIN'S WIFE. Stop being cheeky. She's becoming worse everyday. (*To Girin*) You know, there's something very fishy about all this. One can't really trust these working-girl types, can one?

GIRIN. Well, that's what happens when women stop acting like women.

LILY. Really? And what about when women have to go to work like men?

GIRIN. Shut up, you! All she's ever learnt is cheek.

Girin, who has been getting more and more irate, starts coughing furiously. He gets up from the bed and walks out to the balcony. Shyamal is still there, on the opposite side, smoking. The old man looks at him once, then walks back to his room.

GIRIN. This girl's going to cause you endless heartache, I tell you. Endless heartache.

Cut to Shyamal on the verandah. He leaves the balcony and enters his bedroom. Voices in dispute continue to be heard off-screen.

Cut to Shyamal's wife, who is combing her hair in front of a small mirror hanging on the wall.

Cut to Shyamal as he crosses to a small shelf of books and removes one from the row.

SHYAMAL. Extraordinary! It goes on each day. What's wrong, now? What're the raised tempers all about?

Shyamal walks over to the bed and reclines with book in hand. A baby is sleeping next to him. His wife comes and lies next to the baby, gently caressing the child.

SHYAMAL. Can you hear them? It'll go on all night.

RATNA. But really, what could've happened?

SHYAMAL. Who knows? But they hardly need anything to happen, do they?

RATNA. Oh no, I was thinking of Chinu. It's so late and she hasn't returned home yet. (*She tends to the baby on the bed.*)

SHYAMAL. Oh . . . I don't know. But you know, Ratna, I don't think we should stay aloof in this fashion. We ought to be doing something.

RATNA. Doing what?

SHYAMAL. I don't know . . . make enquiries . . . just stand by them, perhaps.

RATNA. I'm not sure it's a good idea to poke your nose into other people's affairs. They might get upset with you. And in any case, they haven't said anything.

SHYAMAL. That's only because of the embarrassment of it. If something like this had happened to us, I'm sure we'd have done the same thing—not said a word to anyone. After all, we're respectable people. But yet . . .

DWARIK (*off-screen*). Shyamalbabu, the light's still on.

Cut to Shyamal, who looks up in anger and exasperation.

SHYAMAL. So I notice.

Cut to Ratna, who gets up and shuts the open bedroom door.

RATNA (*off-screen*). Shall I switch the light off?

SHYAMAL. No, it'll stay on.

The camera slowly zooms in on the sleeping child.

Cut to the interior of the Senguptas' bedroom. Poltu is sitting up in bed, propped up by pillows, looking at a magazine. Girin's wife is sitting at the foot of the bed. Next to her on the bed is an older woman, a widow. Mother can be seen in the background, listening with a weary expression on her face.

GIRIN'S WIFE. Trouble never comes in ones, does it? The boy splits his head open, while the girl doesn't return home, even at the dead of night. In a little while, of course, all transport's going to go off the streets. When I think of what goes on around here! Why, only the other day they killed a brother and sister in Delhi. My blood ran cold when I read about it in the papers. I'm told that women don't step out at night in those places . . . Not that Calcutta's very different. D'you recall that daylight robbery last week? They broke in and killed the young daughter-in-law before leaving.

Hrishikesh enters the room after politely announcing his presence by clearing his throat. The two ladies sit up and become quiet.

HRISHIKESH. Poltu, try and get some sleep, son.

POLTU. But I don't feel sleepy.

HRISHIKESH. Just lie down, son. Lie down quietly and you'll fall asleep. (*As he picks up a folding chair and goes out to the little porch outside their front door*) You've taken a sedative; if you don't sleep, you'll feel unwell.

He sits near the door, with his back to the camera.

MINU (*to Poltu*). Go to sleep.

GIRIN'S WIFE. It's not that easy, is it dear; you can't fall asleep on order. Moreover, he's closer to his oldest sister than to his mother. (*To the other old lady*) What d'you think?

OLD LADY. Absolutely. He's always been very close to her, even as a child.

MINU. Ma, we haven't eaten as yet.

MOTHER. Why don't you people eat, dear.

MINU. But what about you?

OLD LADY. You can't expect your Mother to eat just yet!

GIRIN'S WIFE. You people should eat . . . and get your father to eat as well.

MINU. Why don't I make the bed?

Minu gets up, walks across the room and picks up a rolled-up mattress with some bedthings inside it.

MINU. I'm afraid I'll be making the bed now.

GIRIN'S WIFE. Of course. We'd better leave; they're making the bed now.

OLD LADY. Lie down for a little while, dear. I'd better be off.

MOTHER. All right then, goodbye.

The two ladies leave the bedroom. Minu drops the bedthings on the floor in a thoroughly exasperated manner. Cut to mid-close-up of Mother. She is looking rather crossly at Minu.

MOTHER. Really! Is that any way to behave with people?

Cut to Minu. She is laying out a bed on the floor.

MINU. Look Ma, stop being so civilized. Those people're behaving as if Didi's going missing all evening's some sort of entertainment. Honestly, this place is a hellhole!

Hrishikesh enters the flat. He is looking as anxious as ever.

HRISHIKESH. Everyone living in the building's found out that our daughter's not returned home yet.

Cut to Mother. She rises slowly, staggers to the table and then breaks down, with her head buried in her arms.

Cut to a stunned Hrishikesh.

Cut to Minu, looking at her mother with a mixture of anger and concern.

MINU. Ma . . . Ma! What on earth d'you think you're doing? Everyone in the neighbourhood'll hear you. What's there to get so worked up about? It's not as if we've done anything. All that's happened is that Didi's rather late returning home. So what? It happens to everyone sometime.

MOTHER. I don't need advice from you people.

MINU. Try and understand, Ma. She might have gone to Srirampur to visit your sister and got stuck there. Or perhaps there's been some problem with the trains, or with the trams and buses, for that matter. Perhaps there was a demonstration, a baton charge, or a bombing. She might even have slipped whilst getting on a bus . . .

Cut to Mother, as she looks up towards Minu, horrified at what has been said.

MOTHER. Minu . . . !

Cut to Minu in mid-close-up, who instantly covers her mouth, looking equally upset at what she has inadvertly said.

Cut to doorway. Topu appears at the door, looking somewhat perplexed and worried.

Cut to low angle shot of Dwarik standing at the balcony, looking down.

DWARIK. Minu, don't forget the front door, will you?

Cut to low angle shot of the facade of the building. It is now in complete darkness.

Cut to close-up of the headlight of a moped, which suddenly lights up. The camera pulls back, to show Amal standing by the scooter, starting it. Topu is standing next to him.

AMAL. Okay, hop on. Where're we going?
TOPU. To the police station first, I should think.
AMAL. The police station? And then?
TOPU. How'm I supposed to tell you that just now?
AMAL. Hmmm . . . We'll have to put in some petrol. Got some?
TOPU. What? Petrol . . . ?
AMAL. Money . . . money . . .
TOPU. Not a lot. But give me a moment . . .
AMAL. Hang on. How much've you got?
TOPU. Oh, about fifty paise or so. But just give me a second . . .
AMAL. Never mind. We'll manage. Come on, hop on.

29

TOPU. The police station, wasn't it?

AMAL. Yes.

The scooter starts. The two young men drive away.

Cut to the exterior of a pharmacy; the camera zooms in on a sign which proclaims OPEN DAY & NIGHT.

Cut to the interior of the pharmacy. It is now recognizable as the one from which Minu attempted to ring her sister's office. The phone rings. A hand slowly rises, gropes for the receiver, lifts it up and puts it down on the table, then disappears.

Cut to Amal and Topu on the moped, speeding through a dark and deserted Calcutta road.

AMAL. Tell me, why're we going to the police station?

TOPU. Well, we might get some information, mightn't we?

AMAL. Whether she's been involved in an accident or something, you mean?

TOPU. Something like that.

AMAL. And . . . ?

TOPU. And whether she's got involved in something else; something very ugly, perhaps.

AMAL. Oh, good grief! What rubbish you talk sometimes. Don't you know your own sister? Don't we all know what Chinudi's like?

TOPU. Nevertheless that's precisely what a lot of people will think.

The scooter approaches and then pulls up at an all night petrol station. They fill up and proceed again, in complete silence.

Cut to close-up of handfan waving back and forth. The camera slowly pulls back to show Minu fanning Poltu. The camera slowly pans right to reveal a worn-out looking Mother, who has dozed

off, then a bone-weary Hrishikesh sitting at the foot of the bed.
Mother wakens with a start.

MOTHER. What time is it? Haven't they returned yet? Oh dear,
that Jhunu's sleeping on the floor.

HRISHIKESH. Jhunu, get up and sleep on your bed.

MOTHER. Why don't you get some sleep as well? It's very late,
you know.

Cut to a high angle shot of Mother, moving Jhunu on to the pillow.
She makes attempts to rise, nearly collapsing in the process. She
rises by making a tremendous effort and manages to stagger to the
door. She holds on to the door and slowly collapses. Hrishikesh
and Minu rise up in alarm.

HRISHIKESH. Are you all right? What's wrong?

Cut to close-up of Minu. She is holding Mother's head in her lap.
Hrishikesh is peering over her shoulder at his wife, panic on his
face.

MINU. Ma . . .

HRISHIKESH. Give her some air.

MINU. Ma . . . Ma . . .

HRISHIKESH. I'll get some water.

MINU. Yes, please . . .

The camera follows Hrishikesh, as he fetches water from the outside tank. He turns back to return to the room.

Cut to close-up of moped, parked on a roadside.

Cut to high angle shot of the street. A jeep comes up and parks at
the bottom of a flight of stairs. A police inspector gets down, followed by a well-dressed young woman and raffish young man. Two
police constables bring up the rear. They climb up the flight of
stairs.

Cut to mid-close-up of Topu, looking on, with trepidation writ large on his face, as the little group pass him by. The Inspector glances at Topu casually as he passes by, then turns and looks at the constables.

INSPECTOR. Put them in the cells.

Cut to a corridor. A sign on the wall announces INVESTIGAT-ING OFFICERS. The camera tracks across an open doorway, showing the interior of an office. Two desks, foreground and back-ground, on screen right. Both desks have inspectors behind them. Amal can be seen sitting in front of the desk in the foreground, with his head resting on his hands. Inspector no. 1 enters and sits in front of the desk in the background.

INSPECTOR 1. God! What a time I've had.

INSPECTOR 2. Why? What happened?

INSPECTOR 1. I've arrested those two smugglers. What a pair! And the queen bee herself, as well.

INSPECTOR 2. The queen bee herself, eh?

INSPECTOR 1. Oh, yes.

INSPECTOR 2. That's great.

INSPECTOR 1. Mind you, you wouldn't guess to look at her. And not a breath of scandal about her.

The first inspector looks around for a cigarette. Amal produces one of his own.

AMAL. Have one of these.

INSPECTOR 1. And what . . . ?

INSPECTOR 2. He wants to make a report. About a missing woman.

AMAL. No, not me. One of the boys from my neighbourhood does. Hold on a moment . . . Topu . . .

Amal gets up and leaves the room in search of Topu.

Cut to close-up of a third inspector, speaking on the phone, in another room.

INSPECTOR 3. Name—Chinmoyee Sengupta. Age—about twenty-five or thereabouts, pretty looking . . . No information? You've not heard anything upto now . . . ? Well, if you do hear anything, let us know, will you? Thanks.

The inspector puts down the phone. The camera follows him to the other room, where Amal and Topu can no longer be seen.

INSPECTOR 3. Well your . . . hey, where've they disappeared to?
AMAL (*off-screen*). Here we are.

Amal and Topu enter the room.

INSPECTOR 3. Right. Look, there's no information as yet. I've enquired at Lalbazar Headquarters, Missing Persons, as well as the Control Room. I've not been able to find out a thing, no one has any information as yet . . . Oh yes, Traffic's sent across a list of deaths from traffic accidents. But your sister's name isn't on the list. She's your older sister, isn't she?
TOPU. Yes.

Cut to close-up of the first inspector.

INSPECTOR 1. Listen, Basak, I tell you what. These people have already made out a report and we're going to be doing whatever's required from our side. In the meanwhile, why don't you give them a letter for the morgue?

Cut to Amal and Topu on the moped. They are driving through a dark street once again. They slowly vanish into the darkness. Slow fade to black.

Cut. Camera slowly pans across the darkness, onto the bed, where Mother is sleeping, next to Poltu. The camera finally comes to rest on a close-up of Mother's face; for once, she is looking in peaceful. Mother wakes up suddenly.

MOTHER. Who's there? Who is it?

Cut to Shyamal's bedroom. He is still reading in bed. Shyamal looks up and checks his watch.

Cut to low angle shot of the house from the courtyard. Shyamal walks across the verandah and comes down the stairs. As he crosses the first floor landing, Naren comes out on the balcony from screen left, hesitates for a moment, then hurriedly follows Shyamal.

Cut; Shyamal crosses the courtyard to the front entrance of the Senguptas' flat.

SHYAMAL. Hrishikeshda . . . ?

Minu comes out of the flat. Faint light can be seen streaming out of the open door.

MINU. Is that you, Shyamalda?

Naren comes and joins the two of them.

SHYAMAL. Yes.

MINU. Have you heard anything? D'you have any news?

SHYAMAL. That's what I came to find out.

NAREN. So there's no information yet?

MINU. No, but Dada's gone to the police station with Amalda, from next door.

OLD LADY (*off-screen*). Is there much point in going to the police?

Shyamal turns around to see who is speaking.

SHYAMAL. What're you doing out here at this hour?

Cut to mid-shot of the very elderly lady, seen once before. She is sitting under one of the many arches on the ground floor.

OLD LADY. Oh, I do this virtually every night . . . the asthma makes me feel as though I'm suffocating, so I come out for a breath of air. They're all sleeping; might as well let 'em sleep.

SHYAMAL (*to Minu*). Where's your father?

MINU. He's lying down for a while, trying to get some sleep.

OLD LADY. That's a good idea, considering what he's going through.

Cut to doorway. Mother can be seen standing there, in mid-close-up.

MOTHER. Who's there? Who's that?

Minu quickly goes to her mother.

MINU. Oh Ma, you're not up again! Didn't I tell you to lie down?

MOTHER. What were you talking about?

MINU. Shyamalda was asking . . .

MOTHER. Shyamal, have you heard anything?

SHYAMAL. No, but we're making enquiries. Don't worry, every-thing's going to be fine . . . get some sleep in the mean time.

MINU. Come and lie down; you're not very well. Come on now.

Minu gently but firmly drags her mother away. As they disappear indoors, Shyamal turns to walk off.

SHYAMAL. Shall we . . . ?

NAREN. Searching for a lone girl in this large city . . . and at this time of night at that . . .

SHYAMAL. Yes, seven million people live here. How the hell can you find anyone here?

The camera follows Shyamal and Naren as they walk back to their rooms. At the bottom of the staircase, they pass young Lily, who is standing quietly in the shadows. They go on their way. The camera remains on Lily. At the far corner of the screen, the old lady can be seen.

OLD LADY. Who's that? Is that you, Lily?

LILY. Yes, Grandma.

OLD LADY. So you're up at this odd hour as well, eh? Here, come and sit next to me . . .

Lily joins the old lady under the arch.

OLD LADY. What happened to the girl? It's so late at night, I just hope that she's not in some kind of trouble. She really slaves for that family of her's, doesn't she? This morning, as she left for work, she told her mother, 'Your cooking stove's got a hole in it. I'll buy you a new stove as soon as I get paid.' If a boy did half as much, everyone'd sing his praises to the high heavens. But since she's a girl, no one says a word. If a boy hadn't returned home so late, people would've worried themselves sick. A girl—and all everyone does is gossip. It's hell to be born a woman.

Cut to moped speeding on its way, through another dark street. close-up of Amal and Topu. Topu's face is seen in profile, looking very pensive.

(Flashback begins.)

Cut to Chinu in mid-long shot standing against a white background. Camera slowly zooms in on her, while the voices of her siblings can be heard off-screen.

TOPU. Hooray! Didi's got her job. The United Commercial Bank. Basic pay, Rupees 190; Dearness Allowance, Rupees 342; House Rent, Rupees 18; City Compensatory Allowance, Rupees 30. Total, Rupees 580. Bloody hell, 580!

POLTU. What fun!

TOPU. Now, you won't forget your unemployed brother, will you?

POLTU. I want a suit.

TOPU. And a dhoti for Baba.

POLTU. And a sitar for Jhunu.

CHINU. Minu, don't you want . . . ?

MINU. What would I want?

CHINU. No more taking tuition for you. You can't do the housework, study and teach others, all at the same time. From
now on, you just concentrate on your studies and help with
the housework.

The zoom ends in the close-up of a happy-looking Chinu, her face
wreathed in smiles. Slow fade to white.

(Flashback ends.)

Cut to dark street, as the moped carries on its way. The street slowly
fades to black.

Cut; Amal is standing by the roadside, smoking a cigarette; two
men pass him by, bearing a rope bed.

Cut to the inside of the morgue. Long shot of a corridor, with two
men standing near a door at the far end. The left wall of the corridor is a bare whitewashed wall. The right wall has a series of metal
doors with heavy handles affixed to it.

Cut to Topu.

ATTENDANT (*off-screen*). Come in, come in . . .

Topu advances, very hesitantly indeed. The attendant opens one of
the metal doors and slides out a shelf, which has a dead body on
it. The body is that of a male.

ATTENDANT. Not this one? I see, you're looking for a woman.
This way . . . a young woman . . . this way . . . not even this
one?

The attendant opens one door after the other, sliding out the bodies
for identification. Topu follows behind, slowly, covering his nose
and mouth with his hand. His eyes have the fixity of a sick fascination; he is obviously revolted by the sight of the cadavers, but

cannot tear his eyes away. The bodies are not seen, after the first one.

ATTENDANT. . . . There's a recent arrival; you'd better check.

The final body is that of a badly injured young woman, with a blood-bespattered face.

Cut to the front entrance of the morgue, in mid-long shot; Amal is in the foreground, looking at the morgue. Topu rushes out, followed by the attendant.

AMAL. Topu, you alright?

Topu rushes past Amal without stopping.

Cut to Topu, retching near a wall.

AMAL. Hey, what's wrong?
TOPU. Nothing. It's okay.
AMAL. Did something happen?
TOPU. No.
AMAL. Topu . . .
TOPU. I just said, it's nothing . . .

Topu continues to retch.

AMAL. Oh hell . . . Topu, Topu . . .

Topu finally stops vomiting and slowly stands up. He then walks up to Amal.

TOPU. Awful, it was absolutely awful. You ever been to the morgue?
AMAL. Not just the once, let me tell you.

Topu retches once again, then rushes off to the same spot near the wall, stoops over once again and starts vomiting. Amal slowly walks towards him, with a rather superior smile on his face.

AMAL. Hell! Bloody old woman . . . he sees a corpse or two and passes out. Oi, you . . .

Amal lightly kicks Topu whilst he is still bent over. Topu rises in absolute fury.

TOPU. AMAL ... !!!

The camera zooms rapidly on to Topu's face, transformed by rage.

Cut to a close-up of Amal, looking vaguely surprised at his friend's anger.

AMAL. Well ... ?

TOPU. Sorry ... Amal, you'd better go home.

AMAL. And you?

TOPU. It'll take me some time yet.

Amal stares at Topu for a few moments, then nods in grudging agreement and leaves on his moped.

Cut to Topu, absent-mindedly rubbing his chest. He still looks shattered by his experience in the morgue. Topu walks back to the corner of the street, as the moped appears once again out of the darkness. As the moped stops, Amal looks back at Topu.

AMAL. Stop acting crazy. Hop on.

Topu climbs on to the pillion of the moped without saying a word. They drive off into the night. Fade to black.

TOPU. Amal ... ?

Cut; camera very slowly pans left on the dark screen, to reveal Hrishikesh sitting quietly by himself. He appears completely preoccupied with his own thoughts.

Cut to a long shot of the lane; it is half lit and half obscured in darkness. A jeep appears at the far end of the lane. Two policemen alight and walk towards the house. In the lead is the officer who had earlier arrested the group of smugglers. He checks the house numbers with the help of a torch

INSPECTOR 1. Chatterjee, this is the house—20A. Come on.

He knocks.

Cut to Minu, hurrying to the front door, after she has switched on a light. Minu opens the front door, the camera staying on Minu in mid-shot.

INSPECTOR 1 (*off-screen*). Does Mr Hrishikesh Sengupta live here?

MINU. Yes.

INSPECTOR 1. Could I have a word with him, please?

MINU. He's not very well. Could I help?

INSPECTOR 1 (*off-screen*). And you are . . . ?

MINU. His daughter.

INSPECTOR 1 (*off-screen*). And Chinmoyee Sengupta . . . ?

MINU. Yes, she's my older sister. I imagine that my brother must've . . . ?

INSPECTOR. That's right, he came to the station. We're here for some information. May we come in?

MINU. Yes, please come in.

Cut to over-the-shoulder shot; the Inspector enters, followed by the constable.

MINU. Did my brother . . . ?

There is a slight noise in the background, as though of a window or door opening somewhere nearby. Minu immediately looks suspicious and closes the door.

Cut to Minu closing the door from inside. She turns. We are in a part of the courtyard that is being used as some sort of lumber room, with broken chairs etc., piled in one corner.

MINU. Er . . . is my sister . . . I'm sorry, but my mother's not too well, either. You won't mind if we talk in this . . .

INSPECTOR. No, no, this is fine. We'll make ourselves comfortable; sit down, Chatterjee. (*To Minu*) Is it all right to sit?

MINU. Yes, of course. Please sit.

INSPECTOR. Could you get me a pen . . . No. It's okay.

MINU. Have you had any news of my sister yet?

INSPECTOR. I'll come to that in a minute. But first, what was your sister wearing when she went to work this morning?

MINU. A printed saree, I think—the colours were cream and violet.

INSPECTOR. And the blouse?

MINU. Ummmm . . . I'm not certain.

INSPECTOR. Any other details?

MINU. Whatever d'you mean, other details?

INSPECTOR. You know . . . handbag, wristwatch, that sort of thing.

MINU. Oh yes, a wristwatch. Yes, she was wearing a watch . . . and she was carrying a black handbag; a shoulder bag to be precise.

INSPECTOR. Is she fair?

MINU. Yes, not like me . . .

INSPECTOR. I'm afraid I'll have to ask you questions about her personal life. I mean, who amongst you would have details of her exclusively personal matters?

MINU. Well, she generally keeps herself to herself. But I suppose she tells me, if she does anyone.

INSPECTOR. Was she intending to go out anywhere, before or even during office hours, d'you think?

MINU. Go out? Who, Didi?

INSPECTOR. Yes, anywhere on the Canning-Diamond Harbour line?

MINU. Why, no. But why d'you ask?

INSPECTOR. Does your sister have any . . . er, men friends?

MINU. Men friends?

INSPECTOR. Well, no . . . er, I mean . . . was she seeing anyone?

Cut to Hrishikesh in mid-shot. He slowly comes up behind the two policemen and listens silently.

MINU. Yes, there was someone.

INSPECTOR. Who?

MINU. Somnath Roy.

INSPECTOR. D'you know him?

MINU. I used to. D'you recall the student–police clashes?

INSPECTOR. Which clashes are you talking about?

MINU. The ones in March '76. The police opened fire during the trouble in College Street. Somnathda was there at the time. He had to be present. He was one of the people killed in the police firing.

INSPECTOR. Ahem . . . Yes . . . Does your sister have a birthmark on her right thigh? A black one?

MINU. I'm sorry, but could you tell me why you're asking these questions?

INSPECTOR. Well, information was received in Lalbazar that a woman had jumped out of a running train near Sonarpur station, on the Canning–Diamond Harbour line. She's now in NRS Hospital. Her condition's not good. Attempted suicide, I should imagine. She was wearing much the same sort of clothes; the sort you described, I mean. And carrying a bag and wearing a wristwatch, just like you said. There was a small diary found on her, without any name or address on it. Just a letter inside. No address there, either. We think it was written to her by some man—perhaps the man who deserted her . . .

Cut to Hrishikesh. He looks absolutely devastated.

Cut to Minu, who is also looking shocked.

INSPECTOR. . . . And she was pregnant. (*As Minu walks across the screen*) Very early stage . . . She's been admitted to the emergency ward of NRS Hospital, bed no. 58 . . . You can go and see her if you want to . . . I'm sorry to have troubled you. (*To Hrishikesh*) You're Hrishikeshbabu, aren't you? Goodbye. Come, Chatterjee.

The two policemen leave, through the door on screen left. Minu hurries to screen left, the camera following her. Close-up of Hrishikesh and Minu standing together, both looking quite distraught, gazing at the departing policemen.

Cut to the police, as they leave.

Cut to Minu and Hrishikesh.

MINU. It's all rubbish! The description didn't match at all . . .

HRISHIKESH. What was that they were saying . . . ? Something about an early pregnancy . . . ?

MINU. No, no, that's nonsense. But you'd better go to hospital anyway. I'll stay with Mother . . . Take Shyamalda with you. I'll call him.

Cut to Minu as she hurries across the courtyard and up the staircase. The camera follows her in a low angle shot, all the way up, to Shyamal's front door.

Cut to a close-up of Shyamal, asleep in bed. A loud knocking can be heard off-screen, causing Shyamal to sit up in bed.

MINU (off-screen). Shyamalda . . .

Shyamal rises and walks to his front door. As he opens the door, Minu can be seen standing outside, looking very anxious.

MINU. The police were here a moment ago. They haven't any definite news, really, but apparently there's this woman in NRS Hospital. In the emergency ward, bed no. 58. I have to stay with Ma and the others. Will you go? To the hospital? With Baba . . . ? Please . . .

SHYAMAL. Yes, of course I will. Give me a moment.

Cut to a close-up of Amal and Topu on the moped. They come to a stop under a portico. Shyamal can be seen at a distance at the end of a corridor, leading off from the portico. He walks up to them.

SHYAMAL. You here, too? How did you find out, anyway?

TOPU. Oh, we'd gone home and they told us.

SHYAMAL. The woman's in a bad way; they're not letting anyone see her at the moment. We've been asked to wait . . . There're a lot of others as well.

AMAL. Others? What d'you mean, others?

SHYAMAL. Lots of other families, is what I mean. Come along.

Cut to a waiting area. The camera pulls back and then slowly tracks left across the room, revealing three anxious-looking people in close-up—a middle-aged man, next to him a man in his late thirties and finally, a widow in her late forties. The camera continues to pan, finally coming to rest on Hrishikesh, sitting next to a man roughly his own age.

BINOD. My daughter? She's more or less the age that's on the police description. In the afternoon she told me that she was going to Sonarpur, on the Diamond Harbour–Canning line. To visit a friend, you know. But she didn't go to the friend. And she hasn't returned home, either.

HRISHIKESH. But you don't know that anything's happened, do you?

The camera now starts tracking back, over the first three faces. We see the widow first, very worried and perturbed. The camera slowly zooms in to a close-up of her face.

WIDOW. It isn't like they say. My daughter's just turned twenty-five. Moreover, why on earth would she want to go to Sonarpur? Still, I had to come; in fear of the police. Mind you, I'd been noticing that something was wrong with her. For the past four days, you know . . .

The camera pans slightly to the right, then zooms into a close-up of the middle-aged man. He looks quite angry.

BENOY. I'm an old- fashioned man myself, so I didn't care much for my granddaughter's ways. One boyfriend today, another one tomorrow—no decency whatsoever. I mean, there're limits to freedom, after all. I knew that it would come to this one day.

The camera continues with its rightward pan, this time onto a close-up of the young man.

ASHISH. Take my sister. We live in the same house. Such a jolly, cheerful person; always fooling around with my youngest daughter. She's very close to the youngest child. This morning she told her that she was never coming back. We thought it was some sort of joke. But . . .

Cut to a close-up of the widow.

WIDOW. If the girl had got herself into some kind of trouble, why didn't she come and tell me?

Cut to a close-up of Ashish.

ASHISH. My sister's a divorcee. Who knows, perhaps she'd made a mistake.

Cut to a close-up of Hrishikesh.

BINOD (*off-screen*). But it isn't possible. My daughter's a widow. That's right, a widow!

HRISHIKESH. Let's wait and see who's unlucky, shall we?

The camera moves back to Ashish, the widow and Benoy, and cross-cuts between them.

WIDOW. No. My daughter's never kept any secrets from me.

BENOY. Jump from a train? I don't believe it. My granddaughter's not capable of something like that.

ASHISH (*with a slight smile*). Perhaps we're all getting a trifle overwrought.

Cut to the corridor leading off from the waiting area. A nurse can be seen approaching. She walks up to the group.

NURSE. Which of you people wanted to see the patient on bed 58? I'm afraid she's dead! She died a minute ago; her injuries were just too severe. We couldn't save her . . .

Shyamal stands up.

NURSE. . . . Can you see the building on the right? The one with the collapsible gate? The body's been sent there; you'll have to go there to identify it . . .

The middle-aged, angry gentleman quietly collapses. The nurse rushes to him and starts attending to him.

NURSE. Get Dr Roy here . . . Please, don't crowd around . . . Why don't you go and identify the body, one by one . . . Please, stop crowding around.

Cut to mid-shot of Shyamal, who walks across to Hrishikesh. Hrishikesh is looking totally lost.

SHYAMAL. Stay here and don't move. Amal, you stay here as well. Topu, come with me.

Shyamal and Topu leave screen left, out of the frame. The camera remains focused in close-up of a dazed-looking Hrishikesh.

Cut to the morgue. Low angle shot of the widow, who enters the frame from screen right. She stops midscreen, looks downwards, slowly nods a 'no' and with a sigh of relief makes an obeisance. The man enters next, looks once, shakes his head and turns his face away. Ashish arrives and looks downwards, almost stunned. Topu and Shyamal quickly pass by, barely glancing at the dead body off-screen. The camera follows the two of them.

SHYAMAL. Tell your father that there's nothing to be worried about. I'll be back in a minute . . .

Shyamal walks back to Ashish, who is still looking downwards in horrified fascination.

SHYAMAL. Your sister?

ASHISH. Yes.

Shyamal looks sympathetic, then quietly leaves him to his grief.

Cut to a dark street. Cars with blazing headlights flash past.

Cut to high angle shot of cityscape at night. The sound of a rotary press can be heard in the background. Various lurid headlines appear on the screen.

WOMAN'S CORPSE FOUND IN THE LAKE.
DISMEMBERED FEMALE TORSO IN TRUNK AT HOWRAH
STATION.
PATHETIC CONFESSIONS OF A CALL GIRL.
EXPOSE OF THE FLESH TRADE.

Cut to close-up of Shyamal. Camera pulls back slightly to reveal the Senguptas' bedroom. Shyamal is looking very thoughtful. A loud ticking can be heard in the background.

SHYAMAL. It's time I went.

Cut to Hrishikesh.

HRISHIKESH. Going so soon?

SHYAMAL. You folks must get some rest. And we're only a
   minute away.

Shyamal rises to leave.

SHYAMAL. . . . Come on, Ratna.

RATNA. Okay, then.

Shyamal leaves the room, followed by Ratna and Minu. The camera reveals an exhausted Mother in close-up, sitting on the floor.

Cut to Shyamal crossing the courtyard. He stops abruptly, as one of the neighbouring ladies appears, followed by others.

SHYAMAL. You people . . . ? What are you doing here?

GIRIN'S WIFE. Is there any news?

SHYAMAL. Why is everyone so agitated? Leave them alone for a while, will you; they might have things to say to one another. Come on, let's go.

The women disappear in different directions, followed by Shyamal.

Cut to Hrishikesh in close-up. The camera pulls back until Hrishikesh is seen in mid-shot. Minu walks into the room from screen right and sits on a chair. The camera pans and then tilts right to show Mother sitting on the floor, propped against the bed. She is quietly dozing.

Cut to mid-shot of Hrishikesh.

HRISHIKESH. God only knows what's happened to the girl.

MOTHER. Minu, didn't she tell you anything at all before she left? Come on, love, don't keep secrets from me?

MINU. For goodness' sake, Ma! Why would I want to keep any secrets from you?

MOTHER. I just know she's never coming back.

MINU. Well, if you know so much, shut up about it.

HRISHIKESH. Minu!!

Cut to Topu, seen in a slight high angle shot.

MINU (*off-screen*). Dada, I believe you threw up after you visited the morgue. Amalda told me you threw up.

Cut to a close-up of Minu. The loud ticking of the clock can be heard.

MINU. . . . Tell me, haven't you felt like puking when you see *this* morgue? This room? This house? . . . (*As the camera pans over each face*) We've never spared a single thought for Didi until now. We've simply carried on like the selfish creatures we are. And today . . . today when she disappears in this fashion . . .

MOTHER. And scuttles us in the process . . .

MINU. Yes, that's what's really important to us, isn't it? That we've been cast adrift. A girl's been suffocating little by little every day, in this room, in this house. And today . . . we're all thinking about her a lot, aren't we?

HRISHIKESH. For God's sake, what are you on about? This is hardly the time to be saying all this.

MOTHER (*agitated*). She's been saying whatever comes into her head for some time now, hasn't she?

POLTU. Stop it, Ma.

MINU. Ma, tell us the truth. Have you ever thought of Didi even once? Even for an instant?

MOTHER. Of course not, dear. You've been doing all the thinking.

MINU. No. We've none of us thought of her. You, me, Baba, Dada, none of us. All we've done is to think of ourselves. And Ma, you've wanted your daughter to stay with you and not leave home.

MOTHER. Never . . .

MINU. Really? Have you ever considered her marrying?

MOTHER. Of course I've considered it. I've often thought that once Topu's settled, we'll marry the girl off.

MINU. Once he's settled, you'll think of Dada's marriage and not Didi's.

MOTHER (*angrily*). Now what's got into you today, Minu? Are you going to tell me that you don't know I've been collecting her wedding ornaments over the years?

As the camera pans over the faces in the room, the following voices are heard.

MINU (*off-screen*). But Didi never wanted all that. All she wanted was to marry Somnathda.

MOTHER (*off-screen*). And what a fine state she'd have been in, if that marriage had taken place.

MINU (*off-screen*). But at least she'd have been fulfilled.

MOTHER (*off-screen*). Fulfilled, is it? And spent her entire life in widow's weeds!

MINU (*off-screen*). Of course, if Somnathda hadn't been in that state, you'd have arranged her marriage with him, wouldn't you?

MOTHER. He didn't even have a roof over his head. He used to spend all his time working for the Party. And he wanted Chinu to earn a living.

MINU. She's doing exactly that even now, Ma.

MOTHER. And where would you be, if she didn't?

MINU. Yes that's it; say that; speak the truth. That actually we needed her.

Throughout this heated exchange, Mother has been getting more and more angry at Minu's scathing comments. She now half rises, in fury, pointing accusingly towards Hrishikesh.

MOTHER. Why're you telling me all this? Tell that man over there, that man sitting so silently.

Cut to close-up of Topu.

TOPU. Will you people just shut up, please?

MOTHER. The only thing he's ever done, is to remain silent; and left all the responsibilities to me . . .

Mother slowly dissolves in tears and slumps to the floor.

Cut to close-up of Topu, grimly looking away from everyone else.

Cut to a close-up of Hrishikesh. He slowly stands up in the midst of the emotionally exhausted group, then silently walks out into the courtyard. A high angle shot of Hrishikesh, standing alone in the middle of a dark courtyard. He sits down slowly. The sound of a fire engine can be heard off-screen.

Cut to a high angle shot of the cityscape at night.

Cut to close-up of Minu.

> MINU. We'll forget Didi. And any relationships that might have existed with the people in the neighbourhood. After all, we'll have to leave this flat and take a cheaper one. I'll have to give up my studies . . . and take up a job. Then, one night, you'll wait for me in the same way. Stay up all night, inform the police, visit hospitals and what have you, and so on and so forth. But I won't return. Like Didi, I'll . . . (*She bites her lip, then rises and sits on another chair next to the window.*) And Didi, even you only thought of yourself. You didn't think of us either. I'd thought of you as somehow different, but in the end you turned out to be as selfish as the rest of us . . . (*She breaks into tears.*)

The camera slowly traverses a shattered and emotionally drained family group, all of whom seem to be locked into their individual silences, with the exception of a distraught and sobbing Mother, with Poltu's hand resting on her shoulder, on whom the camera finally comes to rest. Everyone becomes quiet for a while. The silence is broken suddenly by the sound of a car. Everyone rises, including the injured Poltu. Poltu runs to the window, and looks out over Minu's shoulder.

> POLTU (*excitedly*). Ma, Didi's returned . . . Didi's returned . . .

Jhunu goes to the front door and opens it. The door opens on a smiling Chinu.

Cut to a stony-faced Jhunu, who moves aside without answering. Chinu closes the door on the camera.

CHINU. Why, you're still up. Haven't any of you slept? (*She turns around after shutting the door.*)

Cut to inside the courtyard. The family arrive one by one, to look at Chinu silently. They are all unsmiling and unwelcoming. This is obviously not the reception that Chinu was expecting. She becomes more and more perplexed.

CHINU (*coming forward*). . . . I'm sorry; you must have gone out of your minds with worry. But I got stuck somewhere. I tried to leave a message at the pharmacy but . . . *(She puts a hand on Jhunu's shoulder, but Jhunu moves aside. The expression on Chinu's face indicates that she is very hurt. To Jhunu*) Well? (*To Hrishikesh*) What is it . . . ? (*To Mother*) What's the matter with everyone?

Mother looks at Chinu in a disbelieving and, perhaps, contemptuous manner.

MOTHER. Enough! Let's not make a laughing stock of ourselves in public. Jhunu, come inside.

Mother leaves, followed by Jhunu. Chinu slowly moves to the centre of the courtyard. Minu is watching from a distance. She walks away without saying a word. Topu appears and looks at the people leaving, with some amazement.

Cut to low angle shot of facade of building. The lights on the upper floors come on one by one.

Cut to the courtyard once again.

TOPU. Didi, come inside now.

HRISHIKESH. Go in, will you.

Chinu slowly goes indoors. She halts briefly on the way and looks sideways at Mother in her room, sitting on the bed, with Jhunu close by.

Cut to Poltu, sitting on the bed. He is obviously puzzled by what is happening.

POLTU. What's wrong, Ma?

Cut to Dwarik, looking down from the top-floor balcony.

Cut to the girls' bedroom. Minu is huddled on the bed, staring studiously at the floor. Chinu comes close to her, looking at her sister with a hurt expression.

CHINU. What is it, Minu? Didn't you people want me to return home? (*As she walks to the other end of the room*) Did any of you even wonder about what might have happened? Did you consider that I might have something to say for myself . . . No one asked me anything . . . no one even said anything. In fact, none of you even gave me a chance to say a word. Ma didn't even bother to shout at me! And you . . . Jhunu almost shrank away and Baba just stared at me in that manner . . . D'you people really trust me so very little? (*As she takes a sari from the clothes rack*) Of course, if I'd had an accident you'd have had nothing to say . . . My God! I've become a stranger in just a couple of hours . . .

MINU (*as she looks up at Chinu*). Didi . . . you . . .

Poltu opens the door and looks in Chinu's direction.

Cut to front of house. Dwarik can be seen coming down the stairs.

Cut to Hrishikesh and Topu.

DWARIK (*off-screen*). Hrishikeshbabu.

HRISHIKESH. Sorry, yes?

DWARIK. Could you step this way, please.

Cut to Mother, looking in the direction the landlord's voice comes from. Hrishikesh goes out into the courtyard and stands before Dwarik.

53

HRISHIKESH. Yes, what did you want to say?

DWARIK. Look, whatever's happened is your personal business. I've got nothing to say about it. In any case, this isn't the time to say anything. But really, after all that's happened through the night, I can't remain entirely silent either . . . There are other tenants living here. I've got to see to them as well. I mean, you know what's best for you. But there is one request I'd like to make to you. Please, find another place as soon as you can and leave. This is a respectable neighbourhood, after all . . .

Hrishikesh looks absolutely tongue-tied in embarrassment at the position he has found himself in. Dwarik looks at him once and turns to leave. He comes out on the courtyard.

TOPU. Just a minute. What was that you said?

Dwarik comes upto Topu in a deliberate manner.

DWARIK. I said that this is a respectable neighbourhood. All these disreputable goings on won't do.

TOPU. What the hell d'you mean, disreputable?

DWARIK. Don't you know what disreputable means . . . ?

Chinu comes rushing out from her bedroom, closely followed by Minu.

MINU. Didi, where are you going? Listen . . .

CHINU. Please, please believe me . . . I didn't . . .

TOPU. Didi, go in now.

MINU (*firmly*). Didi, come inside. (*As they go inside*) Sit down here.

Topu turns on Dwarik fiercely.

TOPU. Listen you, if you can't keep a civil tongue in your head—

DWARIK. Civility, eh? You're going to teach me civility, are you?

TOPU. It's not a question of teaching . . .

DWARIK. Then what is it a question of, eh? The girl spends all night in some . . .

Topu lunges for Dwarik and takes him by the throat.

TOPU. You bastard!!!

An ugly scene takes place between Topu and Dwarik, with the latter bearing the brunt of it.

DWARIK. What d'you think you're doing . . .

TOPU. I'll smash your face in, you . . .

DWARIK. Stop it you hear, stop it . . . Help, look everybody, he's attacking me . . .

Cut to Mother. She comes running out and drags Topu away somehow. Topu is still raging, whilst Dwarik is clearly frightened out of his wits. There is general commotion all around.

TOPU. Let me go, Ma . . .

Shyamal comes running and removes a distressed and scared Dwarik from the surrounding chaos. The balconies are all crowded with onlookers.

SHYAMAL. What the hell d'you think you're doing, Dwarikbabu? Topu, stop it this instant, you hear?

CHINU. Ma, come inside. Topu, sweetheart, please . . .

MINU. Didi . . . (*She leads Chinu indoors.*)

Cut to Poltu, staring out of a corner.

Close-up of a furious Topu standing in the middle of the courtyard.

TOPU. So what if he's the bloody landlord, he doesn't own us. Respectability, eh? I'll give him respectability. I'll kick him in his respectable teeth, is what I'll do . . .

Topu storms out of the house.

Cut to Mother as she turns to go indoors. Camera pans left to show Chinu in the parents' bedroom. Close-up of a shattered-looking Chinu.

Cut to Mother, and then Hrishikesh, looking at Chinu.

Cut to Minu, looking at her sister. She comes and stands beside Chinu.

Cut to Chinu.

MINU. Didi . . . ?

Cut to Mother.

MOTHER. Minu, let her get some sleep.

MINU. Didi . . . come on . . . let's get some sleep.

Hrishikesh comes and quietly stands behind Chinu. After a few moments he caresses her head gently. Chinu finally bursts into tears.

Cut to a close-up of Mother. She is desperately trying to fight back tears.

Cut to a close-up of Hrishikesh's face; he, too, is trying to fight back tears.

Cut to a high angle shot of the city. It is early morning.

Cut to the courtyard. People are already busy. Servants are washing up, breaking coal for the stoves etc. Some people are bathing at the outside tank. Mother appears on the ground floor portico, yawning. She arranges her sari over her head in the traditional manner and moves out of the frame, screen left.

Cut to mid-long shot of Lily. Camera follows her as she moves from screen left to right, and finally comes to rest on Mother. The sound of a plane flying high overhead can be heard in the background; Mother is looking upward, following the plane as it flies past overhead.

Cut to close-up of a pair of hands, breaking coal with a hammer. Camera pulls back to show a maidservant breaking coal and behind her, another washing dishes. In the background, a man is bathing with water from the outside tank. In the far background, a woman lights a coal stove. Almost immediately, it starts belching forth grey smoke. The camera pans right slowly and finally comes to rest on the kitchen window. Through the bars of the window, Mother can be seen entering the kitchen.

Cut to the interior of the kitchen. Mother opens the inside door of the kitchen, turns and walks screen right. Music starts.

Cut, as camera tracks across the outside wall of the kitchen and comes to rest on the window. Mother can be seen through the bars. She is sitting in front of the coal stove, attempting to light it. She succeeds in striking a match after several attempts and lights the stove.

Cut to the lit stove outside, which is still belching forth fumes. The camera moves right, to show Lily watching from behind a pillar. Her expression is both concerned and fearful.

Cut to point-of-view shot of the kitchen window. Mother is seen through the bars, in mid-long shot. She is sitting behind the coal stove, her face partially obscured by the smoke. The camera maintains this position for some moments, then slowly zooms in until Mother is seen in mid-close-up. The left half of the screen is obscured by smoke. Mother is seen through the bars, lost in thought and looking as though a great weight is pressing down upon her. The music fades out and the ticking of a clock can be heard for a few seconds. Abrupt fade to black, and the title EKDIN PRATIDIN appears.

Fade to black.

The Case Is Closed

Kharij (1982)

Translated from the Bengali

Credits

Story	Ramapada Chowdhury
Screenplay and Direction	Mrinal Sen
Photography	K. K. Mahajan
Sound Recording	Jyoti Chatterjee
Music	B. V. Karanth
Art Direction	Nitish Roy
Editing	Gangadhar Naskar
Produced by	Neelkanth Films

Cast

Artiste	*Characters*
Anjan Dutt	Anjan
Mamata Shankar	Mamata
Indranil Moitra	Pupai
Debapratim Dasgupta	Hari
Sreela Majumder	Sreela
Nilotpal Dey	Police inspector
Bimal Chatterjee,	
Charuprakash Ghose,	
Binoy Lahiri,	
Ramen Roy Chowdhury	
and others.	

35 mm/normal screen 1.1.33/95 min/Eastmancolor

Dedication to Gene Moskowitz, followed by a list of acknowledgements, unrolling against the blank screen.

Freeze frame of Red Road, Calcutta. The frame is divided in two by the double white lines running through the middle of the road/screen. Lone moped on screen left, mid-ground. On screen right, a car in mid-ground, and four cars in the background. The credits unroll, from bottom to top, over this freeze frame. At the start of the credits, the sound of passing traffic can be heard clearly; halfway through, this is replaced by orchestral music. Frame unfreezes; cars and mopeds rush past in both directions. A man's voice is heard, hailing a taxi.

Cut to interior of cab; driver's upper body is visible, from the back. A couple are having a conversation off-screen, while the street can be seen through the windscreen.

ANJAN. Well then?
MAMATA. Well then, what?
ANJAN. After our marriage . . . ?
MAMATA. Hmm?
ANJAN. What would you like?
MAMATA. What would I like?
ANJAN. Your own flat? A car?
MAMATA. No.
ANJAN. Only sarees?
MAMATA. No, no, no.
ANJAN. Fridge?

MAMATA. Oh, no.

ANJAN. TV?

MAMATA. Not even that.

ANJAN. Well, you tell me.

MAMATA. You don't know?

ANJAN. No.

MAMATA. You mean you really don't know?

ANJAN. No. You tell me.

MAMATA. Mister, I only want you. (*Both laugh.*)

The driver turns abruptly, and looks over his left shoulder, and the shot freezes at this point.

Cut to the interior of a room. A man in his early thirties is shaving in front of a mirror, with an orange towel draped over his shoulders. He is seen from the back; little is visible of his face, as it is covered with lather. He sounds like the man in the taxi, and seems a smug sort of person, obviously quite pleased with himself. A man who hopes to be moving up in the world.

ANJAN. You landed your job just before we got married, whilst I got a promotion within two years. It was your luck, and my efficiency. Now, tell me what you'd like? Your own flat?

MAMATA. No.

ANJAN. Car?

MAMATA. No.

ANJAN. Only sarees?

Mamata turns to him briefly and smiles.

MAMATA. Oh, no.

ANJAN. Fridge?

MAMATA. Uh huh.

Camera pans slowly to the right, revealing first a set of striped curtains, then a door leading to a stairway, and finally the rest of the room, a young woman in her late twenties and a little boy of six or seven. The room belongs to people who are surviving at a middle-class level due to their combined incomes. It is dominated by a bed; next to the door is a table covered by a floral cloth, with an alarm clock on it. One of the walls has a rack, with books etc. on it. The young woman is preparing the little boy for school.

MAMATA. No.

ANJAN (*off-screen*). A radiogram?

MAMATA. No.

ANJAN (*off-screen*). A locker in the bank?

Mamata turns to smile at Anjan.

MAMATA. No, dear. (*As she goes to the table*) What I really need now is a servant; preferably a boy not more than twelve to fourteen years old.

Mamata gives her son a glass of milk.

ANJAN (*off-screen*). Low salary . . .

MAMATA. Don't spill it on your shirt, love.

ANJAN (*off-screen*). Won't eat much . . .

MAMATA. Yes. (*Laughs.*)

ANJAN (*off-screen*). And won't talk back.

MAMATA. Besides, he'll fetch the coal, light the stove, make the tea . . . (*To her son*) Pupai, here love, let me; come and sit here. (*To Anjan*) . . . he'll learn how to make tea (*starts doing the bed*), wash the tea things . . .

ANJAN (*off-screen*). Fetch cigarettes and matches . . .

MAMATA. Yes, and run small errands, do the dusting . . . go to the shops, queue for the kerosene, go to the *dhobi* . . .

ANJAN (*off-screen*). And lose a few clothes in the process . . .

MAMATA. Look after the house whilst we're at work . . . play with Pupai.

Mamata goes up to Pupai, and sitting in front of him, hangs a canteen of water from a strap over his shoulder.

MAMATA. And what else will he do for my darling Pupai? He'll take him to school.

PUPAI. And bring me back . . . ?

Freeze shot of a smiling Mamata.

An over-the-shoulder shot of Mamata approaching the open door. A man is squatting on his haunches in front of the door—thin-faced, slightly grey, smiling in an ingratiating manner. Next to him is a boy of twelve or so, also thin, but very grave and unsmiling. He is dressed in a cheap striped shirt and grey shorts.

> MAMATA. Well, d'you think that you'll be able to manage everything? It's rather a lot of work. (*To Father*) D'you think that he'll manage?
>
> HARAN. Of course he will, ma. All you have to do is show him how. He's a quick learner, my son.
>
> MAMATA. But will he be able to live away from you?
>
> HARAN. And why not? He'll be living with a respectable family, after all.

Camera tilts up, in a point-of-view shot. The man shaving crosses from screen right to left, looking over his shoulder in a rather amused and quizzical manner.

> HARAN. . . . He shouldn't have any cause for complaint.
>
> MAMATA. But look here, the last one left as soon as he learnt the job.

Pupai comes and stands in front of his mother. She ruffles his hair affectionately.

> HARAN. Oh no, I'm sure he'll be very happy with you. Ganesh, from next door, has explained everything. We're from the same village, you see . . .

Cut to the collapsible gate at the top of the stairs. This is moved to one side by yet another boy of twelve or thirteen. He carries two plastic buckets, one yellow and the other blue, across, then shuts the collapsible gate and descends the stairs. At the landing, the two boys look at one another briefly before the second lad carries on down the stairs, a bucket in each hand. The stairway is empty again.

HARAN. There's a famine back home—we've had a severe drought, you know . . . Because he'll be living with you, he'll be getting two square meals, not to mention a salary. As for the work, you've just got to teach him. He's a village lad after all, he can do any kind of work. He'll even carry heavy loads from downstairs—you only have to tell him.

Reverse shot of Mamata and Pupai. She is ruffling his hair affectionately.

MAMATA (*smiles*). Well, he won't have to do anything like that. What's your name, son?

Shot of man and boy. The boy is solemn and unsmiling.

HARAN. Go on, tell the lady your name.

Cut to a grave Palan.

MAMATA. Well, what's your name?
PUPAI. My name is Pupai.

Cut to Haran and then Palan. Palan looks at his father.

Reverse shot of Mamata and Pupai. She laughs, removes the toy that he has been holding, and puts it aside, possibly on the table next to the door.

MAMATA. Put it down. It'll break.
HARAN. My sister named him Palan. She's the one who raised him, after his mother died.

Mamata looks startled and seems a bit disturbed by the news. She looks down at her son intently for an instant.

MAMATA. I see.
HARAN (*off-screen*). He's my youngest.

Mamata looks at Haran directly again.

MAMATA. Yes, well, is it settled then?

HARAN. Won't you increase it by a few more rupees at least? He's only a little boy after all, without a mother . . . and if they didn't need the money very badly, would anyone . . . ?

Cut abruptly to Anjan, sitting inside the room, idly riffling the pages of some magazine, and listening curiously.

MAMATA. In a few months, perhaps. Let him learn the job first. Oh, never mind, let's say thirty rupees.

Point-of-view shot of Mamata, with Pupai just visible in front of her. Palan is standing in front of her, with his father still squatting.

MAMATA. Of course, there'll be new clothes for Puja, and . . . Well, can he stay back today?

HARAN. Of course he can, ma. That's why he's brought all his things with him. (*Haran hands over a small tin trunk to Palan.*) Here we are.

MAMATA. We'll provide his bedthings, so don't worry about those. But by the way, does he have any warm clothes?

HARAN. Warm clothes?

The other boy crosses behind these two, carrying two filled buckets, from screen left to right. He stops for a brief moment at screen right, and continues up the stairs.

Cut to Anjan, still idly riffling magazine pages, whilst listening in.

ANJAN. It's alright, we'll take care of it. (*To Mamata*) Hire him, hire him.

MAMATA. Okay, we'll see what we can do about it. It's just a question of a couple of months, anyway.

In the mean while, the other boy has reached the top of the stairs.

Cut to mid-close-up of Haran and Palan.

HARAN. I want you to know, ma, that I'll be visiting regularly. It's only an hour-and-a-half by train, after all. I'll come each

month and take his salary; he's just a boy after all. You'd better not give him any money.

MAMATA. Very well.

HARAN (*to his son*). Be good, son. Work hard and do what they
tell you. And the young master . . .

Reverse shot of Mamata and Pupai. Pupai is grinning broadly; he
is obviously pleased at the idea of Palan working.

MAMATA. The young master's very naughty, mind you.

HARAN (*to Palan*). . . . You look after him.

PUPAI (*smiling*). Palan . . . !

Freeze for an instant on Pupai's delighted smile.

Cut to long shot from roof of building, camera panning right
slowly, revealing a vista of rooftops. It is a misty morning. Title
appears on screen, saying 'Calcutta, 29 December 1981. Calcutta
in the grip of a cold wave.' The sound of a printing press is heard
in the background.

Cut to interior of bedroom. Anjan and Mamata under a quilt, with
Anjan in the foreground and Mamata in the background. Mamata
yawns, awakens.

MAMATA. What time is it?

ANJAN. It's late. The sun's out.

MAMATA. And you didn't wake me up? I'd promised Pupai that
we'd take him to the zoo!

ANJAN. Shall I wake him up, then?

MAMATA. Let it be. It's too late now. We'll go in the afternoon.

ANJAN. It must be the coldest day of the year!

MAMATA. As far as you're concerned, every day is the coldest day
of the year! You'd better start getting some exercise, or you'll
develop a tummy.

Mamata goes to the bedside table and picks up her shawl, which she wraps round herself before going to the door and starting to open it.

ANJAN. Pass me the matchbox, will you? It's in the kurta pocket.

Mamata crosses to the back of the room and searches various kurtas.

MAMATA. My God! How lazy can you get? Which kurta?

ANJAN. That one over there, the khaddar one.

Mamata tosses Anjan a box of matches, then goes back to the door and starts opening it.

Cut to low angle shot of door from outside, from the bottom of the stairs. Mamata opens the door and comes out on the landing.

MAMATA. Palan . . . Palan . . .

Point-of-view shot, looking down the stairwell. Hari can be seen on the lower landing, rolling the bedding.

MAMATA. Hari, wake Palan, will you, son.

HARI (*looking up*). Palan's sleeping in the kitchen.

Low angle shot of Mamata from bottom of stairs. She looks surprised and moves off screen, to the left.

MAMATA. The kitchen? Why in the kitchen?

HARI. He told me that he felt cold at night.

Cut to Hari, who is carefully putting away his meagre bedding. He places it at one end of an alcove under the stairs, where the boys obviously sleep. The blanket is placed next to a couple of tin trunks, which are raised on bricks. The wall of the cubby hole is decorated with cut-out photos of various film stars, mainly Indian. Hari finishes folding his bedthings and goes up the stairs. Mamata can be heard off-screen, calling out for Palan. As Hari reaches the upper landing, the door opens and Anjan can be seen. He comes out yawning and ambles down the verandah, dressed in kurta and pyjamas, cigarette in hand. He is obviously feeling the cold; stops in front of the kitchen, where Mamata is banging on the door.

ANJAN. What's up?

MAMATA. It seems that Palan slept in the kitchen last night.

ANJAN. Why?

MAMATA. Because he was feeling cold; give him a shout, will you.

Mamata walks back to their flat, looking and sounding quite exasperated.

MAMATA. Put on something warm, will you. It's very cold.

Anjan starts banging on the door.

ANJAN. Palan, Palan . . . hey, Palan . . .

Anjan attempts to wake Palan in a rather perfunctory manner, then casually walks away, clasping his body against the cold. He leans on the parapet in front of their flat, smoking thoughtfully.

Cut to the stairs, where an elderly man is seen ascending. He is well protected against the cold, and is carrying a stick. He stops at the landing. This is the landlord, Benoy Lahiri.

ANJAN (*off-screen*). Back from your stroll eh?

BENOY. Yes.

ANJAN. Cold outside, is it?

BENOY. I should say it is. Makes the bones creak . . .

Benoy starts up the stairs again. Hari is coming down the stairs with a bucket full of garbage. Benoy stops Hari.

BENOY. Hey you, don't you dare leave the rubbish in the middle of the pavement. Why can't you put it on one side? It's almost become impossible to walk on the pavement these days.

Benoy carries on up, Hari goes downstairs. Camera pans right to show the length of the verandah. Mamata comes out of their flat and walks towards the kitchen.

MAMATA. Haven't you woken him up yet?

ANJAN. I've tried. He doesn't answer. I seem to get all the lazy ones.

Anjan walks back to the flat, whilst Mamata carries on with the attempt to wake Palan.

MAMATA. Palan . . . Palan . . . Palan . . . Palan . . . Palan . . . hey, Palan . . .

Cut to stairs. Benoy's wife comes down the stairs, passing screen left to right.

Cut to Samir, coming out of his flat, wiping his face with a towel. Benoy passes by, his back to the camera.

Cut to Mamata, banging away on the door. Anjan comes out again still holding a towel, and purposefully moves to the door.

ANJAN. Well?

MAMATA. He doesn't answer.

ANJAN. Move aside, will you?

Anjan starts banging on the door, while Mamata stands away.

ANJAN. Palan . . . Palan . . .

By now the loud banging has started drawing attention. Benoy comes out on his verandah and peers down. Hari walks across the upper verandah, looking very concerned. An off-screen voice calls out his name and he moves out of the frame. Mamata walks to a different part of the balcony, trying to peer into the kitchen. People are coming out of their flats drawn by the noise.

Cut to Mamata.

MAMATA. Palan . . .

ANJAN. Palan . . .

MAMATA (*as she moves to look from another part of the balcony*).
Even the window's closed. Why don't you bang louder?

Cut to inquisitive onlookers, looking on, and then to an embarrassed Mamata.

ANJAN (*loudly*). Palan . . . Palan . . . (*To Mamata*) Who the hell
told him to sleep in here? This is hardly the place to sleep!

A young man is peering down from the upper verandah, whilst
Hari is scrubbing the balcony on his hands and knees.

SAMIR. What's going on there?

HARI. Palan was sleeping in the kitchen last night.

SAMIR. Why?

HARI. Because he felt cold during the night.

Cut to onlookers.

MAMATA (*off-screen*). Palan . . . Palan . . .

Cut to Samir, hurrying down the stairs, looking perturbed. He
joins the other two.

SAMIR. What's going on here?

MAMATA (*off-screen*). It's Palan. He was sleeping in the kitchen
overnight and won't wake up now.

SAMIR. What . . . ?

Cut to onlookers. Samir joins Anjan at the door, and starts banging
on it.

Cut to Hari, looking on.

Cut to Anjan and Samir, banging on the door.

Cut to Pupai, who has also been attracted by the commotion. Various people, including Benoy's wife, have started gathering.

Cut to Pupai, standing before a locked door. Mamata picks up Pupai.

Cut to Samir and Anjan at the door.

> SAMIR (*to Hari*). Go and get a hammer.
> MAMATA. What're you doing here? You're going to catch a cold.
> PUPAI. What's happening, Mummy?
> SAMIR. Where's that hammer?
> HARI (*off screen*). I'm getting it.

Hari comes down the stairs, puts a bucket down and then rushes towards the kitchen, with a hammer in his hand.

Cut to bedroom, where Mamata is helping Pupai put on a pullover.

> MAMATA. Palan slept in the kitchen last night, and now he's not
>   waking up.

Cut to the landlord's wife.

> PUPAI. Why Mummy? Tell me why?
> MAMATA. You're not to take off your sweater. Don't you know
>   that it's cold outside?

Cut to the landlord.

Samir and Anjan break the kitchen door open, watched by a number of onlookers, including a frightened-looking Mamata standing at her door. An unmoving Palan, covered in a sheet.

> SAMIR. Palan . . . Palan . . .
> ANJAN. Palan . . .

Cut to a frightened Mamata, shrinking backwards.

> SAMIR. What's the matter with him?

ANJAN. I don't know . . . I'll get the doctor, you ring for an ambulance.

SAMIR. Right.

Cut to onlookers.

Cut to Anjan leaving the house. Mamata stops him.

MAMATA. Wait. Take your shawl.

ANJAN. Give it to me, then . . . hurry up, for God's sake.

Anjan rushes off. As Samir gets to the staircase, he is stopped by a
frightened and anxious-looking Mamata.

MAMATA. You are ringing the ambulance service, aren't you?

SAMIR. Yes.

Samir goes upstairs, enters his drawing room, and starts dialing. A
tense Benoy enters behind him, looks at him once and disappears
inside the flat.

Cut to Hari, who enters the kitchen, sits next to the sheet-wrapped
body, and calls out Palan's name softly. Mamata appears at the
doorway, and calls Palan's name in a frightened, strident voice. She
looks very anxious. A perturbed-looking Pupai comes out and
watches.

Cut to a doctor examining the body.

DOCTOR. Would you open the window, please.

Samir opens a window. The kitchen brightens considerably. The
doctor carries on with his examination.

Cut to a long shot from the same roof as before. We are looking
down a Calcutta street on a foggy winter morning. An ambulance
approaches from the background. Camera pans right to follow the
ambulance as it disappears under the corner of the roof.

Cut to street level. The ambulance draws up. A large group of curious onlookers have gathered to watch the ambulance men enter. Some people are peering from a distance.

MAN 1. It's at the Lahiri place, isn't it?

MAN 2. Yes, the Lahiri place.

A group of the inquisitive and the curious have gathered outside the front entrance of the house.

NEIGHBOUR 1. What's going on?

BENOY. Nothing really.

NEIGHBOUR 2. Something's going on. We can see that something's going on.

BENOY. I've just said, it's nothing.

Benoy slams the door on their faces.

NEIGHBOUR 2. Strange man! Why not tell us what happened?

NEIGHBOUR 3. And why shut the door on our faces?

NEIGHBOUR 4. Yes, we're neighbours after all; we're here to help.

NEIGHBOUR 5. It isn't something fishy, is it?

Cut to interior of the house. Benoy is showing the ambulance men where to go. Anjan comes in screen right, and moves up to Benoy.

ANJAN. What was that commotion outside?

BENOY. There's a crowd outside. I've locked the door.

ANJAN. You locked the door!

BENOY (*to ambulance men*). Please, come this way.

Cut to Anjan rushing down the stairs, and opening the front door. The same group of men are still waiting outside.

NEIGHBOUR 1. What's going on?

ANJAN. Well . . . you see . . . the boy who works for us fell ill suddenly . . .

NEIGHBOUR 2. But didn't we hear a door being broken in?

ANJAN. Yes, well . . . I think that he must have locked the door from inside before falling asleep.

NEIGHBOUR 3. Have you informed the police yet?

ANJAN. Who does one call first, the police, or a doctor?

NEIGHBOUR 5. Here, let me through.

ANJAN. Please, don't go in . . . Please . . .

Two men shoulder past Anjan despite his pleas.

Cut to Samir coming out of the kitchen, followed by the doctor. Benoy and others are waiting outside the kitchen. The doctor looks at Benoy and Samir, then sees Anjan coming down the balcony, and goes to him.

DOCTOR. You'd better inform the police.

Cut to close-up of a table with three telephones on it, one of which is ringing.

Cut to a shot of an office, with the three phones on one side, with a desk next to it, a steel cupboard against the rear wall. A policeman enters the room, and picks up a phone, and speaks standing up.

POLICE. Hello . . . yes . . . speaking . . . yes . . . yes . . . yes . . . what was the name? I see . . . what has happened? When did you notice that he was dead? I see . . . I see . . . did you call a doctor? Please hold on a moment . . .

Policeman sits down at the desk, and starts writing.

POLICE. Now would you tell me your name, sir . . . Anjan Sen. And your address? Okay, we'll take care of it.

Cut to an open doorway. A young woman comes out, wrapping a shawl around herself. The camera follows her for a brief while into the street.

Cut to street itself, which is full of people, including a several children of Palan's age.

Cut to different sections of the bystanders. Two men, one grey-haired, in his sixties, the other in his thirties, walk through the crowd. Both have shawls wrapped round them. A majority of the crowd is similarly protected against the cold, but some of the children are only in their shirt sleeves. The two men are walking down the road.

OLD MAN. Well, I'm off then.

YOUNG MAN. I'd better get moving as well. I've got to go to office.

OLD MAN. I don't know why people employ such young children; it's such a responsibility, after all.

YOUNG MAN. You're only saying that because something went wrong. But how often do such things happen?

OLD Man. That's not the point. It's illegal, after all.

YOUNG MAN. Illegal ... immoral ... I know all that. But we can't seem to do without them.

OLD MAN. Why can't we? No, no, there ought to be a serious discussion about it—at the national level.

YOUNG MAN. You mean a seminar? (*Smiles*) And what then ... ?

The two men disappear down the road. Behind them, a police jeep draws up, three policemen, including an Inspector, climb out and make their way into the house amidst the swelling onlookers.

Cut to interior of house. Low angle shot from bottom of stairs. The door to the Sen's flat opens, Mamata, Pupai and Sreela come out. Sreela is holding Pupai's hand.

MAMATA (*to Pupai*). Now, don't you be naughty!

SREELA. Don't worry, Boudi. He likes coming to us. Isn't that so?

She picks Pupai up and starts descending the stairs. The three policemen pass her on their way up. Sreela instantly moves aside.

SREELA. Come on, love.

Cut to Sreela and Pupai walking down the street, still full of bystanders.

PUPAI. Why are the police here?

SREELA. Oh, just like that.

PUPAI. Why just like that?

SREELA. Because Palan was naughty, that's why.

PUPAI. But Palan was ill.

SREELA. Well, if you're naughty you fall ill, and if you're ill, the police come and catch you.

Cut to shot of balcony, seen from inside the kitchen. A part of the kitchen is visible. On the left is a table with a hurricane lantern and some plastic utensils on it. Under the table is a bucket. The wall next to the table has a rack hanging from it, containing utensils. On the right of the door is a vacuum flask, hanging from a hook. The Police Inspector and Anjan walk down the balcony and stop at the kitchen door. Hari can be seen between them, standing some distance away. The Inspector carefully looks around the kitchen, whilst questioning Anjan in a clipped but very neutral voice.

INSPECTOR. What did the doctor say?

ANJAN. Well . . .

INSPECTOR. Was the door shut?

ANJAN. Yes, bolted from the inside.

INSPECTOR. Are you certain?

ANJAN. Yes, absolutely. We had to break in.

INSPECTOR. Who is 'we'?

ANJAN. Mr Lahiri and myself.

INSPECTOR. Mr Lahiri?

ANJAN (*to Hari*). Call Mr Lahiri . . . (*To Inspector*) He's our landlord's son.

The Inspector enters the kitchen, carefully steps over the body and continues to examine the kitchen carefully. Various point-of-view shots of the kitchen, showing utensils, then a gas cooker connected to its cylinder, and lastly, a coal stove with ashes scattered around it at the boy's feet.

Cut to the Inspector's feet dodging over Palan's body. The Inspector completes his preliminary examination of the room. He looks at the stove and then at the gas stove. He sounds polite but quite suspicious.

INSPECTOR. What do you cook on, gas or coal?

ANJAN. Both.

Cut to the Inspector squatting in front of the stove, which he examines quite thoroughly.

INSPECTOR. The coal stove seems to have been used last night. I see that the ashes haven't been cleaned as yet. It was put out, was it?

ANJAN. Well, there was no reason for it to have been kept lit, but—

INSPECTOR (*gets up and looks backwards at Anjan*). But what? Go on.

ANJAN. Well . . . it was very cold last night. Perhaps he kept it lit to warm the room . . .

INSPECTOR. Oh . . .

The Inspector continues to look around. He looks up at the ceiling carefully.

INSPECTOR. There's not even a single ventilator in the room, I notice.

Benoy, who has in the meanwhile been listening from nearby, quickly comes to the door.

BENOY. It's not a bedroom after all, just a kitchen.

INSPECTOR. Are you the landlord?

BENOY. Yes, I am.

The Inspector notices a pile of dirty dishes, then looks downwards, presumably at the body.

INSPECTOR. I see that he hadn't done the dishes.

ANJAN. So I notice.

INSPECTOR. I'm afraid that we'll have to take them with us. That plate, was it his?

ANJAN. Most probably.

INSPECTOR. Pandey, take these things to the van. And the bedding—we'll have to take that as well. Now, is there somewhere we could sit?

ANJAN. Yes, of course. Please come this way.

The Inspector and Anjan leave the kitchen, and walk towards the flat. An extremely tense and anxious-looking Mamata is standing at the door.

ANJAN (*to Mamata*). Can you unlock the door?

Mamata enters the bedroom, passing a distraught Hari seen through the bars of a window. She takes a key out of a desk drawer, and hurriedly opening the door, enters the sitting room.

MAMATA. Please give me a minute.

Cut to Mamata, as she tidies the room up somewhat. This room contains a sofa set, with a striped cloth spread over it to keep out the dust, a black-and-white TV set on a table in one corner, a small cabinet containing some china objects against a wall. Mamata lets Anjan and the Inspector in. Benoy enters as well, whilst Mamata leaves the room, picking up a glass ashtray from the table. As she leaves, Samir enters.

Cut to Mamata walking back to the bedroom. Onlookers are gathered all around.

INSPECTOR. So you're the landlord, is that right?

BENOY (*off-screen*). Yes.

INSPECTOR. And your name is . . . ?

BENOY (*off-screen*). Benoy Chandra Lahiri.

INSPECTOR (*off-screen*). And the address? No, never mind, I have the address here. (*To Anjan*) What did you say the boy's name was?

ANJAN (*off-screen*). Palan.

INSPECTOR (*off-screen*). Palan what?

ANJAN (*off-screen*). Can't tell you, I'm afraid.

Mamata returns to the sitting room, carrying the glass ashtray. There are various people standing on the balcony, all doing their best to eavesdrop. Samir is standing by the door. Mamata joins them.

MAMATA (*as she places the ashtray in front of the Inspector*). I'm afraid I can't even offer you a cup of tea.

INSPECTOR. Don't worry about the tea. Please, sit down, I've got a few questions for you as well ... Did you use the coal stove last night?

MAMATA. Yes. The coal stove is used for cooking at night.

INSPECTOR. Who does the cooking?

MAMATA. I do, mostly. I do as much as I can on the gas stove before going to work. I don't use the gas in the evenings.

ANJAN. As you know, gas ... (*To Samir*) Please, sit down ... (*To Inspector*) ... is hardly available freely.

Cut to Inspector looking sideways at Anjan. Mamata, Anjan and even Samir look frightened and quite tense during the interrogation.

INSPECTOR. When did you last enter the kitchen at night?

MAMATA. Let me see ... (*To Anjan*) When did we have dinner last night? ... (*To Inspector*) It must have been around 10 or 10.30.

ANJAN. Yes, it was about 10.30. We went to bed soon after.

INSPECTOR. ... And the boy, he hadn't eaten till then?

MAMATA (*looking at Anjan*). ... No ...

INSPECTOR. And was the stove still burning?

MAMATA. ... Uh ... yes. (*She looks hesitant and guilty.*)

INSPECTOR. Why?

MAMATA. I . . . I'd put a pan to simmer on the low heat . . .

INSPECTOR. A pan? On a *chullah* . . . ?

Cut abruptly to the kitchen, where the Inspector examines the stove, and then peers inside a dish. An anxious trio of Anjan, Mamata and Samir watch him like hawks. A few neighbours are seen walking down the stairs hurriedly. The Inspector comes out of the kitchen and everyone walks down the verandah.

INSPECTOR. I have to ring headquarters. Is there a phone here, somewhere?

SAMIR. There's one in our flat. Please come upstairs.

INSPECTOR. The body has to be sent to the morgue.

SAMIR. Yes, please come along.

As they proceed to the stairs, they pass Hari. The Inspector looks enquiringly at Hari, then pauses near the foot of the staircase.

INSPECTOR. Who's he? A brother?

SAMIR. No, he works for us.

ANJAN. The two of them used to sleep under the stairs.

INSPECTOR. I see.

ANJAN. You know, the room where we were sitting . . . the previous servants who worked for us used to sleep in that room, you know . . . the sitting room, I mean . . . none of them stayed very long anyway . . . there was one boy . . . (*To an embarrassed-looking Mamata*) . . . When did that Prasanna business take place? . . . (*To Inspector*) Anyway, that boy, Prasanna, used to work here. But one day he absconded with some things from that room. And since then we've become rather suspicious . . . (*trails away into silence*).

INSPECTOR (*to Samir*). The phone. Shall we go?

The Inspector and Samir go upstairs, leaving a distraught Mamata and a rather guilty and embarrassed-looking Anjan behind. Anjan looks at Mamata, who rushes into the flat. Anjan turns and follows.

Cut to Anjan entering flat. Mamata is leaning against the shutter of the window, sobbing softly. Hari can be seen through the window, walking past. Onlookers can be spotted in the far background.

ANJAN. What on earth are you doing? You're not a child. Try and understand . . . It wasn't really our fault . . . Listen, for God's sake, it was just an accident . . .

Mamata turns and leans against the edge of the shutter. She is still crying; her face is tear—streaked.

MAMATA. What am I going to tell Palan's father? Please tell me, what am I supposed to say to him?

Both look shattered. Mamata continues to lean against the shutter, sobbing softly. Anjan looks at her a moment and then walks away. The camera follows Anjan. As he crosses the open door towards the other end of the room, Hari can be seen looking through the open doorway. His face is set and cold.

Cut to onlookers on the street. The Inspector, Anjan, and a few other policemen emerge through the crowd and walk up to the police van.

INSPECTOR. So, you were saying that the boy's father comes here pretty often?

ANJAN. Yes, he comes to collect the salary.

INSPECTOR. Send word to his father or somebody. Someone or the other will be needed. And you also come to the thana in the afternoon. The post-mortem report should be ready by then. Well, I'm off, then. (*As the jeep prepares to leave*) Pandey, have you taken the bedding, dishes etc.?

PANDEY (*off-screen*). Yes.

The jeep moves on.

Cut to onlookers, and then Hari, standing next to a wall and looking on pensively.

Cut to a doctor's surgery. Anjan is waiting, along with a number of other people, while the doctor examines a child who is sitting on his mother's lap. Anjan looks very thoughtful as he puffs on his cigarette.

DOCTOR. Now then, open your mouth, son. Let's have a look— that's it . . . (*To Mother*) What's his name?

MOTHER. Ashok.

DOCTOR. Ashok what?

MOTHER. Ashok Ghosh.

DOCTOR. I'm prescribing a powder . . . dissolve it in warm water and make him gargle with it three times a day . . . Make sure he doesn't swallow it. I'm also prescribing a tablet; give him half a tablet three times a day, though not on an empty stomach. Let me know how he fares. (*After she pays him, to the others*) Please excuse me. (*To Anjan*) Come inside, Anjanbabu.

Anjan and the doctor enter his consulting room. The doctor sits on the couch, whilst Anjan sits, at a somewhat lower plane, on a stool.

DOCTOR. Please sit down. Well, there's nothing to be done other than wait for the post-mortem report.

ANJAN. Yes, they asked me to call at the police station sometime this afternoon.

DOCTOR. Quite. You ought to get it either today or tomorrow.

ANJAN. What's your opinion about the case?

DOCTOR. I must say, it's an unnatural death.

ANJAN. Unnatural?

DOCTOR. Of course.

ANJAN. But what about some other illness?

DOCTOR. No.

ANJAN. I mean, one hears of so many strange infections these
days . . .

DOCTOR. No, I don't think so. (*Puts a hand on his shoulder*) In
any case, there's no point in worrying about it now.

ANJAN. You mean the post-mortem?

DOCTOR. Yes. It's out of our hands now;

ANJAN (*looks up, startled*). Umm . . . ?

Cut to interior of bedroom. Mamata is making the bed, while
Anjan is sitting at the table, doodling. Mamata finishes making
the bed, and sits on it. Both are very tense, and avoid looking at
each other. Guilt is obviously eating at them both.

ANJAN. You needn't have told them about it.

MAMATA. About what?

ANJAN. The business about the stove—that you hadn't put it out.
It wasn't necessary at all.

MAMATA. Why, did they say anything about it?

ANJAN. What could they say? You'd already said everything that
there was to say.

MAMATA. But I do that every day.

ANJAN. But he didn't sleep there every day. Didn't you notice
how they were peering inside the pans?

MAMATA (*as she prepares to sit on the bed*). But that's the water I
boil every day for the washing. In any case, what would you
have liked me to say? That I carefully put the stove out? Or
perhaps that I had fed Palan before going to bed?

Cut to Anjan, looking at Mamata briefly.

Cut to Mamata, seated on the bed, shaking her head bitterly.

Cut to doorway. Hari enters carrying a tray, with two cups of tea
and a plate of biscuits on it.

HARI. Boudi?

ANJAN. Ummmm?

HARI. Madam sent this.

Hari offers a cup of tea to Anjan, who takes it but refuses the biscuits. He then offers a cup of tea to Mamata.

MAMATA. Thanks, but I don't want any.

ANJAN. But you haven't had anything all morning.

MAMATA. I don't feel like anything.

ANJAN. Well, since they've taken the trouble to send it, you might as well have the tea.

MAMATA. I said I don't want anything. (*To Hari*) Take it away.

Hari leaves. The couple sit in an angry and uneasy silence. Abruptly, Anjan gets up and leaves the room.

Cut to rear balcony, where Mamata appears out of the bedroom door. Pupai's voice can be heard in the distance, Anjan joins her after a while, lighting a cigarette.

PUPAI (*off-screen*). Mummy, here I am. I won't go to your place. There're policemen there.

SREELA (*off-screen*). Tell them—I've been invited to lunch.

PUPAI (*off-screen*). I've been invited to lunch.

Cut to Sreela's rear balcony, where she is holding Pupai up.

SREELA. Tell them—You've been invited too.

PUPAI. You've been invited too.

SREELA. Say—They've cooked for you as well.

PUPAI. They've cooked for you as well. (*To Sreela*) What have they cooked?

Mamata and Anjan have been listening to this with faint smiles on their faces. Mamata looks around, to see that various people are staring at them through their windows. She makes a moue of disgust.

MAMATA. Look how they're staring. God, how I hate it!

She angrily enters her bedroom, following Anjan, and then slams the door shut.

Cut to shot of the roof, revealing part of the roof and a dense tangle of other roofs, closely set together. Camera slowly pans right, to show Hari leaning against the parapet. He looks very sad and pensive. He turns as an off-screen voice calls his name.

Cut to interior of bedroom. Mamata is applying a dressing on Anjan's finger. Anjan is sitting in front of the dressing table.

MAMATA. When did you hurt it?

ANJAN. While breaking the door open, I imagine.

MAMATA. You should've put something on it then and there.

She finishes and sits on the bed. Both look very much under strain as they carry on their conversation.

Intercutting mid-close-up shots of the couple.

ANJAN. Did you ever tell him to sleep in the kitchen? Palan, I mean. Well?

MAMATA. No.

ANJAN. You never told him?

MAMATA. I just told you, no.

ANJAN. Not even the once?

MAMATA. Why this cross examination, suddenly?

ANJAN. One can hardly sit in that room, much less sleep in it. It doesn't even have a ventilator, for God's sake.

Cut to the stairway, where Benoy is seen to be standing.

BENOY. Anjanbabu?

ANJAN (off-screen). Who is it?

BENOY. It's me.

Benoy walks to the doorway, as does Anjan. Mamata is still sitting on the bed; both she and Anjan look very uncomfortable. Benoy makes no attempt to come in.

BENOY. Hadn't we better inform the boy's father? He has to come and settle things himself.

ANJAN. There's nothing left to settle. Everything . . .

BENOY. No, no, no. The case won't be settled without the father. It is a police matter, after all.

Cut to Mamata on the bed.

ANJAN (*to Mamata*). Do you have it? The address?

MAMATA. No, I don't.

BENOY. Just look for it, I'm sure you've got it somewhere. He was an outsider after all, even though he was living with you. You can't not have his address! Please, I suggest you look for it.

Cut to close-up of Mamata.

MAMATA. His father used to visit regularly, so I . . .

BENOY. But that was only once a month, to collect the salary. You've got to think of accidents and so on, haven't you?

ANJAN. Why don't you look? Perhaps you've got it written down somewhere.

MAMATA. I've already said that I haven't got it.

BENOY. You haven't got it! Good Lord, weren't you even afraid of theft?

Cut to close-up of Anjan.

ANJAN. Perhaps Ganesh might . . .

MAMATA. That's right.

BENOY. Who's Ganesh?

MAMATA. He used to work at Sreela's. He's the one who told us about Palan; they were from the same village. Hold on, I'll ask Sreela.

ANJAN. No, you stay here. I'll go to their place and get the address.

Anjan hurries out of the room. At the doorway he meets Hari, who is quietly standing there. Anjan says 'Well?' in a cursory and enquiring manner and leaves the room.

Cut to outside the doorway, with Hari standing out on the balcony and Benoy glaring at him from just inside the door.

BENOY. What're you doing here?

HARI. I've come for the cups.

Benoy snorts in disgust and leaves.

Cut to inside the room, as Hari enters and collects the cups. Mamata is seen gazing at him.

Cut to living room, Sreela's flat. This is the residence of people who are very much more affluent than the Sens. It is a much bigger room, better furnished, and altogether much more elegant. Anjan is sitting on an armchair, looking tense and distracted, with Pupai next to him. Sreela's grandfather enters the room, from screen right, buttoning his kurta.

SREELA'S GRANDFATHER. There's no point in worrying about it in this manner; what's done is done. Worrying isn't going to bring him back. You've got to bear up, young man. It's only going to be a problem for a few days. Bouma!

He walks out of the room, still doing up his kurta. Sreela enters from screen right and comes and sits next to Anjan. Anjan is seen sandwiched between her and Pupai; Pupai and Sreela, who are sitting on the floor, are both at a lower plane than Anjan, who is looking rather worried.

PUPAI. What does 'problem' mean?

SREELA. Problem means illness.

PUPAI. Illness?

SREELA. Palan was naughty and that's why he fell ill.

PUPAI. Yes I know; Palan was caught and put in hospital.

SREELA. So, what happens when you're naughty?

PUPAI. You fall ill.

SREELA. And if you're ill, the police catch you and lock you up—

SREELA AND PUPAI. . . . in hospital.

Anjan watches Sreela and Pupai's horseplay. He looks clearly irritated as they burst into peals of laughter.

Cut to Sreela's grandfather's bedroom. He is having a conversation with Sreela's mother as he finishes dressing. Again, the bedroom is much better furnished than the Sens'.

SREELA'S GRANDFATHER. It's a strain on the girl.

SREELA'S MOTHER. I know; but we can't let Pupai stay in that house. He must be kept occupied for the time being.

SREELA'S GRANDFATHER. She's had to skip office today.

SREELA'S MOTHER. A day or two won't make a difference. Moreover, he likes being with Sreela.

SREELA'S GRANDFATHER. Oh well, let's go . . .

Cut to Sreela's grandfather and mother coming out of the bedroom into the corridor, where Anjan is waiting for them. Anjan is seen standing before them in the background, and Sreela, who is carrying Pupai, is in the foreground. Sreela, Pupai and Anjan are standing with their backs to the camera.

Cut to Anjan.

SREELA'S MOTHER. Anjan, shall I have your food sent across, or—

SREELA. No, they'll eat here.

PUPAI. Yes, we'll eat here.

SREELA'S GRANDFATHER. That's right, you can eat here. (*To Anjan*) Shall we go?

The two men leave.

Cut to Sreela and Pupai.

SREELA. Come on, let's say goodbye to them.

Sreela walks to the balcony, carrying Pupai.

Cut to the front of the building; Sreela comes out on the balcony, still carrying Pupai. The two of them look downwards, and Pupai starts waving out. Camera tilts downwards, to reveal the front of the building, where the two men are standing, gazing upwards. Both wave out to Pupai, and walk down the road, the camera following them.

SREELA'S GRANDFATHER. Don't worry, I'll take care of Ganesh. After leaving us, he took a job in an office at Moulali. I'll send someone to him immediately and make sure that the boy's father's informed by tomorrow morning.

ANJAN. You are sending him, then?

SREELA'S GRANDFATHER. Of course. How long does it take by train? A couple of hours? If I can, I'll send him today itself.

ANJAN. That'll be wonderful . . .

By now they have reached Sreela's grandfather's car. He opens the rear door. Anjan takes out his wallet.

ANJAN. . . . Can I give you some . . .

Sreela's grandfather turns around and waves away the money that Anjan is offering.

SREELA'S GRANDFATHER. No, that won't be necessary; I wouldn't worry about it . . . okay, I'm off then.

Sreela's grandfather gets into his car and the driver drives away.

Cut to balcony, where Pupai is still waving out frantically, held up by a laughing Sreela.

Cut back to car, driving away. After going a few yards, however, the car stops, and Sreela's grandfather pokes his head out of the rear window. Anjan walks towards the car.

SREELA'S GRANDFATHER. Anjan, by the way, d'you know any good lawyers?

ANJAN. Why do you ask?

SREELA'S GRANDFATHER. Because it's essential to get some legal advice in such matters.

ANJAN. Legal advice? Why?

SREELA'S GRANDFATHER. Well, even though it was a genuine accident, I doubt that the courts would let you off easily.

ANJAN. But I'm afraid I don't know any lawyers.

SREELA'S GRANDFATHER. You don't? Alright, when I get back from office this evening, we'll go and meet a friend of mine. We used to be students together. Have you heard of Benoy Shome?

ANJAN. But he's a big shot!

SREELA'S GRANDFATHER. Yes, he is. But he's also an upright and sound man. Anyway, be ready.

The car drives away. Anjan turns to walk off.

Cut to a group of five young men, sitting outside a house. They are very much the sort of young men one finds chatting at street corners in all the middle-class areas of Calcutta. They are in their early to middle twenties, look rather rough, and are most likely unemployed, since they are idling the morning away. They stand up as Anjan walks away, and the one in the middle calls out. He seems the leader of the group.

YOUTH 1. 'Scuse me, but can we have a word?

Cut to Anjan, who turns around at being called. He looks clearly irritated at being accosted in this manner, but also seems rather wary. The group of five young men walk up to Anjan. The young man who called out is in the middle of the group, and reaches Anjan first. The others come up and virtually surround Anjan.

YOUTH 1. Can you tell us what happened?

Cut to a very concerned-looking Sreela watching from her balcony.

YOUTH 2 (*off-screen*). Something like this happens in our neighbourhood, and we don't even know about it! Can you imagine that?

ANJAN. Well . . . I mean . . . you know, at my house . . .

YOUTH 2. Yes, yes, we knew him . . .

ANJAN. Palan, you mean? Well, he was with us for a year . . .

YOUTH 3. Yes, but what happened, exactly?

ANJAN. Er, my wife was half asleep when . . .

YOUTH 3. Died on the spot, did he?

YOUTH 4. 'Course he did. Didn't you notice them bundling him off to the morgue?

ANJAN. Well, when we found him . . .

YOUTH 5. Informed his parents, have you?

YOUTH 4. Why don't you let him finish?

YOUTH 1. And stop talking rubbish.

YOUTH 4. Please, go on.

Sreela appears. Camera follows her as she walks past behind the group, obviously trying to overhear the conversation. She still looks very concerned. The camera remains on Sreela.

ANJAN (*off-screen*). His mother's dead, he has one brother. We're trying to reach his father.

VOICE 1(*off-screen*). You were saying . . . how did he die?

ANJAN. In his sleep, it would seem.

VOICE 2 (*off-screen*). Seem?

VOICE 3 (*off-screen*). What did the doctor say?

VOICE 4 (*off-screen*). You call that quack a doctor? (*This comment is met by general laughter.*)

Sreela has reached the front entrance of Anjan's house.

Cut to the little group.

YOUTH 2 (*to Sreela*). 'Scuse me, could you get us a glass of water?

Anjan is standing with his back to them; he looks very annoyed at the lot of them. The young men look rather triumphant, particularly the one who spoke to Sreela; he has a huge leer on his face. Anjan is visibly checking his rage.

ANJAN (*to Sreela*). Go inside. (*To the youths*) Why don't you people come in?

Sreela disappears into the house. The youths smile amongst themselves.

YOUTH 1. Shall we?

ANJAN. Yes, please do.

They all turn and walk in through the front entrance of the building, with Anjan leading the way, and the first young man following closely behind. A high angle shot shows us the entrance lane for the first time. This is a narrow lane, about wide enough for two people to walk side by side, bounded by the building on screen right, and a high wall on screen left. The young men bringing up the rear are all talking loudly and at the same time.

Cut to close-up of hand holding a jug of water. The camera pulls back to show Mamata inside their bedroom, pouring water into a tumbler, Sreela is standing beside the door. Mamata looks absolutely livid.

SREELA. I was watching them for a while. They were all sitting there. God only knows what they want . . . Let me . . .

MAMATA. No, I'll do it. It's okay.

Cut to the sitting room. Anjan is sitting with the entire group of young men, looking rather strained. The young men seem quite oblivious to their surroundings. Mamata enters carrying a tumbler of water on a saucer. She hands it over to Youth 2, who drinks it and returns the glass to Mamata. He leaves the saucer on the table, however.

YOUTH 3. Boudi, may I have some water as well?

ANJAN. Why don't you ask Hari to do it?

MAMATA. I can manage, thanks. (*To youth*) Would you pass me the saucer, please?

Mamata leaves the room.

Cut to Mamata entering her bedroom. She looks and sounds entirely fed up, as she goes to the jug to pour out some water. Sreela is still standing near the table, idly looking at a magazine.

MAMATA. As if we hadn't anything to do! Now another one wants a glass of water.

SREELA. Oh, that's just an excuse.

MAMATA. I know.

Mamata upends the jug, then sets it down with a disgusted look.

MAMATA. Damn! Now, we don't even have any water.

Mamata walks out of the room, carrying a half-filled tumbler of water. The camera pans to show the staircase, with Hari coming down, just as Mamata is at the door.

MAMATA. Hari, please fetch me some water, would you, son. The pitcher's in the kitchen.

Hari nods and carries on. Mamata walks down the balcony towards the sitting room. The voices from the sitting room can be heard off-screen.

1ST VOICE. No, no, sir; the old man's an absolute skinflint. D'you know how much he donated for the Puja? . . . How much was it?

2ND VOICE. Four annas.

1ST VOICE. Yes. After making us wear out our soles, he gave us four annas.

Cut to balcony. Hari walks towards the stairs carrying a pitcher of water. The camera pans left to follow him up the stairs. As Hari goes up the stairs, Samir comes down. The camera pans right, to follow him as he walks across the verandah, partway to the Sens' door.

SAMIR. Anjanbabu . . . Anjanbabu . . .

Cut to the Sens' sitting room. A low angle, mid-close-up of a worried and irritated-looking Anjan and Mamata. Anjan is sitting down, whilst Mamata is standing next to him. Both are looking distinctly unhappy, particularly Mamata. Anjan rises at being called, and leaves the room.

Cut to balcony, as Anjan emerges from the sitting room. He comes up to Samir.

SAMIR. What are they on about?

ANJAN. Oh nothing . . . you know . . . just asking . . .

SAMIR. Should I stay?

ANJAN. You're on your way to work, aren't you? You'd better carry on. Not much point in everyone missing their day's work

Samir turns and leaves. Anjan walks back to the room. Glances at Mamata as she comes out of the room.

Cut to the bedroom. Mamata is still annoyed.

MAMATA. I do wish that they'd leave. There was really no need to have invited them in the first place.

SREELA. Dada didn't invite them in, you know.

MAMATA. Well, couldn't he have avoided them?

Mamata and Sreela are sitting side by side on the bed.

SREELA. No, he couldn't have.

MAMATA. I can't even stand being in the same room with them
... The fact is that everyone's taking advantage of our situation ... everyone.

Mamata and Sreela sit in a moment's silence, Mamata with her
head down, and Sreela looking at her sideways, with a certain
degree of apprehension mixed with sympathy.

ANJAN (*off-screen*). Do you hear, they're leaving.

Mamata rearranges her smile and rises.

Cut to the outside landing. Low angle shot from the bottom of
the stairs shows that the young men and Anjan are standing outside the door. Mamata appears at the door, with a patently false
expression on her face.

YOUTH 1. We're off then, Boudi. We shan't bother you anymore
today. But we'll come back another day for tea.

The first youth walks down the stairs, grinning to himself.

YOUTH 3. . . . and some snacks as well.

The rest of the youths follow behind the second speaker. Anjan
follows.

Cut. Low angle shot of Benoy peering from the upper landing.

Cut to a view of the stairs. Benoy comes downstairs, as Anjan
strides up the stairs. Anjan tries to walk past Benoy, who is not
willing to have any of it.

BENOY. D'you realize what you just did, Anjanbabu, asking that
lot into the house?

Hari passes between Benoy and Anjan, nearly bent over by the
weight of the full pitcher of water that he is carrying. Benoy looks
at Hari with a disgusted expression on his face.

BENOY. . . . You don't know what's in their minds. You should've
said goodbye to them on the doorstep.

Cut to Anjan entering the bedroom. Sreela and Mamata are looking quite perturbed. Anjan walks to the far end of the room.

ANJAN. I didn't ask them in . . .

Cut to mid-close-up of Sreela. She looks quite astonished at Anjan's statement, then turns to look at Mamata.

Cut to Anjan, who turns around on reaching the far end of the room; he is standing next to Mamata. Once more, he has an expression of mixed annoyance and guilt on his face.

ANJAN. And even if I did, what of it? Have we committed a theft? Anyway, you could have come down once; it is your house, after all, you do have some responsibilities, or don't you?

BENOY. Responsibilities? What responsibilities? I've rented the house out, and that's all. That's where it ends.

Benoy gesticulates vigorously in refutation of any attempt to make him responsible in any way, for anything. He then turns and walks up the stairs, still nodding his head, and muttering. The camera tracks to the right, and we see Benoy through the bars of the window, climbing up to the landing and disappearing to the left.

BENOY. I have no responsibilities, none at all, none.

Cut to an unbelieving Anjan, and Sreela behind him.

ANJAN. What an extraordinary man! Now he's putting all the blame on us . . .

Anjan comes and sits down next to the table, picks up the alarm clock and looks at it.

ANJAN. What time is it?

Cut to Sreela, who again looks at Mamata, who refuses to meet her eyes.

ANJAN. You forgot to wind it, I presume?

Everyone is avoiding everyone else's gaze.

Cut to balcony of Sreela's flat. Sreela and Pupai are playing a game of tag. They are quite obviously having a merry time. Sreela enters her sitting room, closely followed by Pupai.

Cut to interior of the sitting room. Anjan and Mamata are sitting side by side on two armchairs, idly leafing through magazines. The camera pans to follow Sreela and Pupai's horseplay, then zooms back to show Anjan and Mamata observing them. They look wryly amused.

SREELA. Pupai, can't catch me; come and catch me . . . Pupai,
    can't catch me, can't . . . can't . . . miaow, miaow, miaow!
    Come on . . . and now, a nursery rhyme.
SREELA AND PUPAI (*off-screen*).
    Miss Molly had a dolly
    Who was sick, sick, sick
    So she phoned for the doctor
    To be quick, quick, quick.
PUPAI.
    The doctor came
    With his hat and his bag,
    And he knocked on the door
    With a rat-a-tat-tat.

    He looked at the dolly
    And he shook his head
    And told Miss Molly
    Get her straight to bed.
SREELA AND PUPAI.
    He wrote on the paper
    For a pill, pill, pill.
    I'll be back in the morning

With my bill, bill, bill.

Lala la lala la lala la la la . . .

Mamata has a rather strained smile on her face; she rises abruptly, and walks out of the room.

Cut to the dining room, where Sreela's mother is laying out the table. Mamata comes and stands next to her. Sreela and Pupai enter the room behind her. Pupai climbs up on a chair, and promptly picks up something to eat.

SREELA'S MOTHER. Come in.

MAMATA. Can I do anything?

SREELA'S MOTHER. No, everything's done.

MAMATA. But you've made so many things . . . !

SREELA'S MOTHER. No, not really; just these few things . . . Pupai darling, come and sit here.

MAMATA. But you've gone to so much bother.

SREELA'S MOTHER. It was no bother at all.

SREELA. Oh yes, it was a great bother.

MAMATA. Well, you had to miss work today.

SREELA. So? You couldn't go to office, either.

The sound of the phone ringing can be heard in the background.

SREELA'S MOTHER. Sreela, the phone . . . and ask Anjan to come and eat, please.

Sreela walks out of the dining room door.

Cut to the sitting room. Anjan is still sitting in his armchair, holding a magazine.

ANJAN. Shall I answer the phone?

SREELA. I'll do it, thanks. Mother wants you to come and eat. Hello . . . yes . . . yes . . . what . . . oh . . . then . . . Yes, they've arrived . . . No, we haven't started eating yet . . . D'you want to talk to him? Okay, hold on . . . I'll call him.

Sreela puts the phone down. Pupai has sneaked in behind her, however. She kisses him on the head and leaves the room. He comes to the phone and picks it up.

PUPAI. Hello, hello, hello . . . are you Grandpa? How're you, alright? This is Pupai.

Cut to the dining room door. Sreela and Anjan enter in a hurry. The camera pans to follow them, as Sreela reaches the phone and picks Pupai up. He has a merry grin on his face. Anjan picks up the receiver.

SREELA. You rascal!

ANJAN. Hello . . . speaking . . . what . . . oh!

As Sreela turns and leaves the room, Mamata enters. She looks distinctly concerned, as she comes to stand next to Anjan.

Cut to Pupai and Sreela.

PUPAI . What is it?

SREELA. Never you mind. Let's go and eat.

Cut to dining room. Sreela enters, carrying Pupai. She puts Pupai down on the chair he had climbed on previously. Pupai promptly picks up something from one of the dishes, and starts to eat.

SREELA'S MOTHER. Who's calling?

PUPAI. Grandpa.

Sreela's mother gazes at Pupai fondly for a second.

SREELA'S MOTHER. Is something the matter?

SREELA. Ganesh can't be located. He's not in his office.

SREELA'S MOTHER. Now don't tell me he's left this job as well?

Cut to Sreela's grandfather's office. He is in a room which he shares with just one other person. They are at a good distance from one another, suggesting that this is a fairly spacious room.

SREELA'S GRANDFATHER. No . . . no . . . why would he leave this
job? An office-boy's job is a pretty good job, you know. He's
taken two days' leave . . . What? Ganesh's address? D'you
want it? Yes, I've got it. Write it down . . . it's in a maze of
lanes . . . you'll have to look for it . . . Yes, here we are.

Cut back to Anjan and Mamata. He gestures to Mamata for a pen
to write the address with. Mamata finally gets a biro that works.

ANJAN. Yes . . . go on . . . hold on a moment . . . go on . . . yes,
okay.

Anjan puts the receiver down and turns to look at Mamata. He
looks as anxious as she does.

MAMATA. Now what?

ANJAN. Ganesh isn't in his office . . . he couldn't be found . . . he
hasn't come to work today . . .

Anjan looks as angry as he has ever done through the morning.
He rises and walks past Mamata, who also looks very upset.

ANJAN. . . . No, no, it was very wrong of us.

Cut to mid-close-up of Mamata, who looks somewhat surprised.

MAMATA. What was?

Cut to Anjan, in mid-close-up. The camera pulls back slightly as
he walks across the room, and sits down in an armchair near a window. He cannot even bear to look at Mamata, apart from once, out
of the corner of his eyes.

ANJAN. We should have noted Palan's address . . . this boy was
with us for a long time . . . we had a responsibility . . .

Cut to Mamata. She looks utterly disgusted and angry at Anjan's
self-righteous comment.

MAMATA. It was my responsibility, was it? You could have written
it down as well!

Cut to Anjan. High angle shot of him as he turns in the chair to glare at Mamata.

ANJAN. That's not the point. Who could or who couldn't . . . (*Louder and off-screen*) that's not the point . . .

Mamata is about to tell him to speak softly.

Cut to mid-close-up of a distressed Mamata. The camera rapidly pans right, to show Sreela's mother entering the room.

SREELA'S MOTHER. Mamata, shall we eat . . . ?

Anjan rises and leaves the room. The camera lingers on Mamata, who stands where she is for a few moments. Sreela's mother looks at her for a while and then leaves the room. She seems very near to tears. She puts the biro she has been holding all this while on the centre table and follows the other two out of the room.

Cut to close-up of the rear right wheel of a Calcutta State Transport Corporation bus, travelling at fair speed.

Cut to point-of-view shot of a filthy, wet and miserable shanty lane. A hooded figure. The camera zooms in slowly on a locked door. The shanty the door belongs to stands at the head of the lane, which turns right in front of it. An elderly man peeks out from the corner, looks at Anjan carefully, then comes out to him.

OLD MAN. Who are you looking for? Ganesh, is it?

ANJAN. Yes. Is he not in?

OLD MAN. He's gone to his village . . . something to do with his land. He should be back tomorrow.

Anjan frowns in disappointment and anxiety.

ANJAN. Tomorrow?

OLD MAN. So he said.

ANJAN. Would you happen to know the name of this village?

OLD MAN. I don't, I'm afraid. But I think you have to go by way of Guptipara.

ANJAN. You're certain you don't know the name of the village?

OLD MAN. Yes, quite certain . . .

Anjan turns and walks away, looking rather dejected.

Cut to the old man, peering questioningly at the retreating Anjan.

OLD MAN. . . . Can I take a message?

Cut to the interior of a Calcutta bus. Anjan in mid-close-up, sitting next to a window, looking very preoccupied. He looks up in a startled manner when the conductor approaches.

Cut abruptly to the interior of the police station. Anjan and the Inspector are walking down a corridor in mid-shot.

INSPECTOR. We found a cinema ticket in his shirt pocket. He'd gone to the 9 p.m. show . . . which means that he must have got home around midnight.

ANJAN. Last night?

INSPECTOR. Yes. Why?

ANJAN. Well, where did he get the money?

INSPECTOR. They're never short of money, are they?

They enter an office, the policeman entering first. He sits behind the desk.

INSPECTOR. . . . Come in, please sit down . . . Well, after returning so late, he must have barely managed to bolt something down, before dropping off. Which is why he mustn't have found the time to do the dishes . . .

The Inspector takes out a packet of cigarettes. He takes one himself and extends the packet towards Anjan.

INSPECTOR. . . . Cigarette?

Anjan takes a cigarette. They start to light their cigarettes.

INSPECTOR. . . . Tell me, did any of you feel ill after last night's
meal?

Cut to Anjan lighting a cigarette, in mid-close-up. He looks quite
taken aback by the query.

ANJAN. No. But why d'you ask?

INSPECTOR. No reason, really . . . I was just thinking . . . did you
cook separately for him?

ANJAN. We all ate the same food in our family . . . By the way,
what about the post-mortem report?

INSPECTOR. It hasn't been done yet. But it ought to be ready by
tomorrow. Please come to the police station tomorrow. And
please . . . bring one of his relatives along. Otherwise you
won't get it.

ANJAN. Get what?

INSPECTOR. The body.

Anjan stands up abruptly, in shock. His face looks anguished.

Montage of shots of Palan working, alternating with shots of Pupai
and an older boy playing. Montage starts with a shot of Pupai and
the other boy playing on a slide, while Palan draws water from a
handpump. Next Pupai and his friend are playing on a swing,
whilst Palan breaks coal into useable lumps with a hammer.
Another shot of Pupai and his friend on swings, this time side by
side, while Palan puts a mattress out to air. Ends with a mid-close-
up of Palan leaning against the roof parapet, looking downwards,
weariness etched on his face. He turns abruptly, as we hear his
name being called off-screen.

Cut to the interior of the Sens' bedroom. It is evening, the room is
dimly lit. Mamata is reclining in bed, turning the pages of a drawing book. There is a noise in the background and Mamata turns
around to look.

MAMATA. Who's there?

Cut to the doorway. Hari is standing at the door.

MAMATA. Oh, Hari. Switch on the light, will you, dear . . .

Hari switches on the light, and remains standing silently by the door. He looks very gravely at Mamata.

MAMATA. Did you want to say something?

HARI. I . . . I . . . I know where Palan's village is.

Mamata rises in surprise and excitement.

MAMATA. You do? Why haven't you said anything until now?

Cut to Hari, who remains unmoved by Mamata's fairly sharp query.

MAMATA (*off-screen*). Well?

HARI (*as he comes towards her*). I'd gone with Palan to his village on one occasion.

MAMATA. How did you get there?

HARI. By train.

MAMATA. D'you think you could go again on your own?

HARI. Yes.

MAMATA. To his house?

HARI. I'm sure I could.

MAMATA. There you are. Hey, listen.

Cut to the stairway. High angle shot of Anjan climbing the stairs, looking quite weary. Mamata quickly walks up to him as he enters the room.

MAMATA. Hari was saying he knows.

ANJAN. Knows? Knows what?

MAMATA. Everything . . . Palan's village, how to get there and everything. He's even been there once.

Anjan seems quite unaffected by this news. He looks at Hari once.

ANJAN. Good. (*To Hari*) Run along now. (*Back to Mamata*) Where's Pupai?

MAMATA. With Sreela. Do you want something to eat?

ANJAN. No.

Anjan walks over to the chair beside the bed, and sits down. Mamata sits on the bed close to him. She looks quite animated after talking to Hari. Anjan looks bone weary.

MAMATA. We could send Hari, couldn't we?

ANJAN. And what would he tell them? Do we know how he died? Well, do we?

MAMATA. Didn't they say anything?

ANJAN. Who?

MAMATA. The police. You did go to the police station, didn't you?

ANJAN. They don't know anything as yet . . . at least if he'd died of some illness . . .

MAMATA. Perhaps he was ill; we just didn't know.

ANJAN. That would have made it so much easier . . . we'd know and also understand . . . we'd have something to tell people. But the way he died . . . it's our shame. Thousands of people asking thousands of questions. D'you know what they asked me at the police station?

MAMATA. What?

ANJAN. They asked me whether we cooked separately for him.

MAMATA. Why on earth would they want to know that for?

ANJAN. Presumably because they suspect us of having poisoned him.

Mamata literally recoils physically at this suggestion.

MAMATA. No-o-o . . .

Cut. Anjan and Sreela's grandfather are sitting in the lawyer's consulting room. This is the room of an extremely successful professional man. It is a large room with opulent furnishings, much silk and marble, and a desk of a size befitting the room. The walls are lined with what look to be expensively-bound law books. The lawyer, Benoy Shome, looks the part; he is a pipe-smoking, grey-haired, middle-aged man. All the three protagonists are seen in mid-close-up or occasionally in mid-shot. Shome lights a pipe.

SHOME. You see, the point is that negligence is an offence.

SREELA'S GRANDFATHER. He's our neighbour. I've never seen him neglect anyone. (*To Anjan*) Well . . . ?

ANJAN. He used to . . . I mean . . . He was like a member of the family.

SHOME. No, he wasn't. He was not. Nor was it possible for him to have been so. (*A guilty-looking Anjan and Sreela's grand-father are seen.*) You were fond of him, that's all. Nothing more . . . the advantages that you have, that you can afford, that your son, for instance, obtained; what part of those did he get? (*Anjan is seen, head bowed.*) Did he have a room of his own to sleep in? No he didn't. He used to sleep under the stairs, or in the kitchen. Take this cold wave, for instance. Did you even once consider giving him some warm clothes, or an extra blanket? No, you didn't. None of us ever do . . . How long had he worked for you?

ANJAN. For nearly a year.

Cut to Sreela's grandfather.

SHOME (*off-screen*). Did he ever fall ill?

ANJAN. He got us worried, on one occasion.

SHOME. Oh, he got you worried, did he?

ANJAN. Er . . . I mean, he was ill once.

SHOME (*smiling sarcastically*). And where was he sleeping then? Under the stairs? . . . Tell me, didn't you feel uncomfortable?

SREELA'S GRANDFATHER. Of course he did. But, on the one hand, we have to have servants; and on the other hand, we have neither the space nor the money to house them. So you tell me, what does one do?

In the background, a man can be seen typing, with his back to the camera.

SHOME. That's precisely what I was saying. Didn't this gentleman just say that he was like a member of the family? That's just talk. (*The man who was typing comes and hands over a piece of paper to Shome.*) Do we give them their legal rights, or acknowledge any moral claims they might have? No, we don't, we can't . . . How old was he?

ANJAN. Who, the boy? Twelve or thirteen, I suppose.

SHOME. In other words, a minor.

SREELA'S GRANDFATHER. But it was his father who brought him here. He wanted him to work.

SHOME. What choice did he have? At least there'd be a salary each month, and the boy would get two square meals a day.

ANJAN. But was it our fault, really? I mean, you tell me . . .

Cut to Sreela's grandfather and then Shome.

SHOME. If you look carefully at anything, at anything at all, you'll find the whole world's at fault, morally. And we lawyers . . . d'you see those law books? We suppress the moral truth with those law books. The legal lie must prevail over the moral truth . . . Anyway, let's see what the post-mortem says.

Anjan looks quite shattered after this. He and Sreela's grandfather get up to leave, when Anjan hesitates.

ANJAN. You know, if there'd been just one ventilator in the room.

SHOME. So you've already said. Well, you're trying to save your own skin. However, I'm sure that your landlord's not sitting by idle, either.

Cut to row of pictures on the wall.

Cut to close-up of a successful-looking middle-aged man and Benoy, entering an office. The doctor hangs up his jacket.

DOCTOR. I don't think it's a case of asphyxia . . .

THE CASE IS CLOSED

The doctor turns and sits behind his desk. He motions to Benoy to take a seat. This is the office of a successful professional man, and looks it.

DOCTOR. . . . I'll speak to Dr Ganguli on the phone . . . Sanat—

The secretary/receptionist arrives.

DOCTOR. Sanat, please get Dr Ganguli on the phone—44 5158.

mid-close-up of the doctor, with Sanat's hand dialling the number.

DOCTOR. From what you've just said, it sounds like a case of carbon monoxide poisoning. If carbon monoxide accumulates in an unventilated room, it can be extremely dangerous.

Cut to Benoy, who looks very perturbed on hearing this.

Cut to a pair of fingers, dialling.

Cut to mid-close-up of doctor.

DOCTOR. But you know, the joke is that this carbon monoxide, which combines with our blood, is some two hundred times more potent than oxygen, which is our source of life. (*To Sanat*) Couldn't you get him? Here, let me try . . . (*To Benoy*) In cases of carbon monoxide poisoning, the individual just dies in his sleep, quite unaware of anything . . . (*On the phone*) Hello, could I speak to Dr Ganguli . . . He's not in? Could you call his daughter to the phone? (*To Benoy*) This Dr Ganguli was one of my students; very brilliant fellow— my favourite student, as a matter of fact. But what does he go and do? He starts cutting up corpses. That's why I call him the corpse doctor . . . (*On the phone*) Hello, Shipra. I believe your father isn't in and you don't know when he'll be back. But when he returns, will you please tell him to

109

ring me? Where? Just one moment. (*To Sanat*) Check how
many people are waiting, will you?

SANAT. About a dozen people, sir.

DOCTOR. Hello, Shipra, I'll be at my rooms until ten. After that,
I'll be at my residence. Yes, positively . . . no . . . no . . . it's
not anything serious at all. Thank you, thank you, my dear.

Cut to the interior of the Sens' bedroom. Pupai is asleep and
Mamata lying on her side by him, resting her head on her hand
and looking at him very tenderly. She gets up all of a sudden.

Cut to the stairs. Anjan can be seen in a high angle shot, ascending
the stairs.

Cut to interior of the room. Mamata hurriedly calls Anjan inside.

MAMATA. There you are at last.

ANJAN. Why, what's up?

MAMATA. Come inside.

Anjan steps inside the room and then stops again. He is exasperated. Mamata walks to the bed and sits down.

ANJAN. Would you please tell me what's going on?

MAMATA. He's here.

ANJAN. Who is?

MAMATA. Palan's father.

Anjan is very surprised at this news. He paces up and down rest-
lessly.

ANJAN. My God! When did he arrive?

MAMATA. In the evening, soon after you left.

ANJAN. But who informed him?

MAMATA. No one. He came on his own. D'you realize what day
of the month it is?

Anjan looks over his shoulder. Point-of-view shot of the table by
the window, with the calendar on it. The calendar shows the 28th
as the date.

Cut to Anjan walking to the table. He picks up the calendar and starts correcting it.

ANJAN. Couldn't you even change the date on this thing? Where is he?

MAMATA. In the kitchen.

Anjan moves the curtain slightly to peer at the kitchen once, then walks back to stand in front of the still-seated Mamata.

ANJAN. Have you told him yet?

MAMATA. No.

ANJAN. You mean he doesn't know yet?

MAMATA. He does; Hari told him. He met Hari downstairs.

ANJAN. And then?

MAMATA. Hari informed me.

ANJAN. And then?

MAMATA. I haven't met him as yet.

ANJAN. But why?

MAMATA. I just couldn't!

ANJAN. You mean you ...

MAMATA. And what was I supposed to have said to him?

ANJAN. Oh, nothing, nothing at all. I'll tell him, after all it's my responsibility, isn't it?

Anjan gesticulates angrily and walks away, to stand facing the wall by the head of the bed. His back is turned towards Mamata, who is now sitting turned away from him. Anjan looks over his shoulder towards the bed.

Cut to a point-of-view shot of the sleeping Pupai.

Cut back to Anjan, now looking over his shoulder at Mamata.

ANJAN. Does anyone else know he's here?

MAMATA. I'm sure that the people upstairs do.

ANJAN. Did they come down?

MAMATA. No.

ANJAN. Did you give him something to eat?

MAMATA. No.

ANJAN (*loudly*). Not even a cup of tea . . . ?

MAMATA. Hari's been taking care of him . . .

Cut to the kitchen, seen from the outside. Haran can be seen in mid-shot, sitting on the floor with his head resting on his knees. There is an untouched cup of tea beside him. He raises his head and looks at the camera. His expression is totally grief-stricken.

Cut to point-of-view shot of the bedroom door, seen from the kitchen. The curtain is pulled aside, and Anjan appears. He slowly walks down the balcony towards the kitchen. He walks halfway down and then stops to look towards the bedroom door. Mamata appears and joins Anjan where he is standing. Anjan again walks towards the kitchen, with Mamata following behind him. He stops, and looks towards the interior of the kitchen.

Cut to interior of the kitchen. Low angle shot from inside, with Haran in left foreground, and Anjan standing just outside the door. Mamata is standing near the corner of the balcony. Haran is still sitting with his head buried between his knees. Anjan enters the kitchen, stands next to Haran, gently touches his head and calls his name. Haran bursts into sobs with his head still lowered. Anjan continues to stroke Haran's head, and squats next to him.

Cut to Mamata, who is quietly crying outside.

Cut back to kitchen.

ANJAN. Haran . . . it happened so suddenly . . . we . . . we . . .

Haran now breaks into inconsolable sobs.

HARAN. Please . . . please, give me my Palan back, please . . .

Haran continues to sob, his head touching the ground near Anjan's feet, in a gesture of almost total submission.

Cut to high angle shot of upper half of kitchen door. Mamata can be seen, slightly blurred, crying in the balcony. Anjan rises to stand against the door, as if he needs its support. He is almost wincing in pain.

Cut to Haran, head on the ground, crying. Anjan's legs can be seen behind Haran. Mamata is in the background, crying.

Cut to the Sens' sitting room. mid-close-up of Mamata sitting next to Sreela's grandfather. She is sitting with her head down, hugging herself, almost as if she is huddling against something. Sreela's grandfather lights a cigarette. Sreela reaches across the coffee table and puts an ashtray in front of him.

> SREELA'S GRANDFATHER. He's obviously in dire need; that's why he came to get the salary a few days early. Just as well, I suppose.

Mamata looks at Sreela, rises, walks to the window, and closes it.

Cut to Sreela's grandfather, puffing away on his cigarette.

> SREELA'S GRANDFATHER. Sreela, what was that you were saying? The boy had come to see you?

Cut to Sreela and Mamata, with Sreela in mid-close-up and Mamata standing behind her.

> SREELA. Yes, last evening.
> MAMATA. Who did? Palan?
> SREELA. Yes. He came to ask me for two rupees.

Cut to mid-close-up of Anjan.

> ANJAN. And did you give him the money?

SREELA. Yes.

Cut to Sreela and Mamata. They are both where they were. Mamata is looking curiously towards Anjan. Mamata then walks over to stand by the wall shelves.

ANJAN. Hmm . . .

MAMATA. Well, what is it?

ANJAN (*off-screen*). He went to the cinema last night.

MAMATA. He did? Who told you?

Cut to Anjan and Sreela's grandfather.

ANJAN. The police. They found the stub of a ticket in his pocket; for the 9 p.m. show, it was.

Cut to Mamata. She looks towards Sreela, screen left.

MAMATA (*to Sreela*). Did he tell you that he was going to the cinema?

SREELA. Not in so many words. But . . .

Mamata is looking quite angry now.

MAMATA. You shouldn't have given him the money, you know.

Sreela looks rather crestfallen at this comment.

MAMATA. . . . Recently, he'd been keeping very bad company.

Cut to Anjan. He looks up at Mamata.

Cut back to Mamata.

MAMATA. The fact that he borrowed money from you is of no great consequence. But only the other day, he brought home a pair of shorts and said that the lady from one of the houses in the neighbourhood gave it to him. (*A guilty-looking Sreela comes into view.*) . . . People are hardly that charitable these days . . . it feels awful; as if we never did anything for him. As if we never showed any sense of responsibility . . .

Cut to mid-close-up of Sreela's grandfather. He carefully stubs out his cigarette.

MAMATA. Didn't we provide him with whatever he needed?

Cut back to Sreela's grandfather and Mamata.

SREELA'S GRANDFATHER. Well, it's all over now. There's not much point in recriminations . . .

He gets up and walks towards the door opening on to the balcony.

SREELA'S GRANDFATHER. . . . Isn't this north wind freezing?

Mamata bites her lip in an attempt to hold back her feelings and then rushes out of the other door. As she leaves, Mamata passes Samir.

SREELA'S GRANDFATHER. Sreela, you'd better go and . . .

Sreela passes Samir.

Cut to the bedroom. Mamata is standing silently, still biting her lower lip. She looks very distressed. Sreela enters behind her.

SREELA. Boudi, I'm sorry that I gave him the money without asking you.

Mamata seems to flinch in embarrassment.

MAMATA. Sreela, I never meant . . . please sit down.

Sreela sits down on the bed. Mamata sits down on the chair next to the bed. As she sits down, the camera tilts to show the stairs, seen through the bedroom window. Mrs Lahiri, the landlord's wife, is coming down the stairs. The camera pans to show the door of the bedroom. Mrs Lahiri is standing at the door.

MRS LAHIRI. Mamata . . . ?

Cut to Sreela and Mamata. Mamata looks over her shoulder at the door.

MAMATA. Please, come in.

Cut to Mrs Lahiri, who enters the room and sits down on the bed next to Sreela. She looks downwards towards the bed.

Cut to point-of-view shot of the sleeping Pupai.

Cut to Mrs Lahiri and Sreela in mid-close-up.

MRS LAHIRI. He hasn't dropped off to sleep on an empty stomach, has he?

SREELA. No, my mother fed him.

Cut to Mamata in mid-close-up.

MRS LAHIRI. You'll eat at our place tonight.

MAMATA. Thank you . . . and his father?

MRS LAHIRI (*off-screen*). And his father as well, of course . . . What a terrible thing . . . such a happy boy, always cheerful . . . just goes off to sleep and dies! You're both at work, so you wouldn't know . . . but I used to see him . . . You've no idea how difficult Pupai used to be at meal times . . . Palan would follow him all over the house in order to make him finish his meal. He really was fond of Pupai . . . It's very hard to look his father in the face. Imagine, the poor man'd come to collect his son's wages! You know, he used to bring a little gift every time; I'm sure he's brought one with him again . . .

Mamata has been looking more and more uncomfortable during Mrs Lahiri's comments. She is no longer able to contain herself, and rushes out of the room.

Cut to the sitting room. Anjan and Samir can be seen in the background, sitting on a couple of armchairs. In the foreground is

Sreela's grandfather, in mid-shot. He is pacing up and down, looking at the two younger men over his shoulder.

SREELA'S GRANDFATHER. So you're saying that the post-mortem report'll be available tomorrow?

SAMIR. That's what Father said.

SREELA'S GRANDFATHER. He contacted them, did he?

SAMIR. Yes.

SREELA'S GRANDFATHER. Good . . .

He stops pacing about and sits down on an armchair.

SREELA'S GRANDFATHER (*off-screen*). . . . I was wondering; since the father's here, hadn't we better ask him to stay back?

ANJAN. But he wants to return . . .

SREELA'S GRANDFATHER. Naturally he does . . .

SAMIR (*off-screen*). He won't get a train at this hour, though.

SREELA'S GRANDFATHER. Besides, now that he's here, we mustn't let him go. We've got to keep an eye on him.

Cut to Anjan and Samir in mid-shot. Samir is nodding in agreement, while Anjan seems doubtful.

ANJAN. Hmmm . . .

SAMIR. That's very true.

Cut to Sreela's father in mid-close-up, sitting on the armchair.

SREELA'S GRANDFATHER (*off-screen*). One never knows, but people might put ideas in his head; there's no shortage of such people . . .

At this moment, the camera gradually tilts up to the window. We see Haran through the window, coming out of the kitchen and slowly walking towards the sitting room. He looks dazed and broken, but seems to have heard what is being said in the sitting room.

SREELA'S GRANDFATHER (*off-screen*). We must prove to him that Palan's death was an accident and quite outside our control . . . that such incidents happen regularly in our country and they happen because of us . . . although from what the doctor said . . . By the way, the doctor said that carbon monoxide poisoning . . .

Haran has reached the door of the sitting room by now.

Cut to mid-close-up of Anjan, who notices him at the door.

ANJAN. Come in. Take that seat . . . won't you sit down?

Haran enters the room rather cautiously; grief-stricken, he looks at everyone in the room, before squatting on the floor, near the door, next to Sreela's grandfather. He looks as though he is unable to comprehend what is going on.

HARAN. I think I had better go home. My family doesn't know anything about this.

SREELA'S GRANDFATHER. You can't, any longer. There's no transport available at this hour. Instead, tomorrow morning we could . . .

SAMIR. . . . Yes, we could send Hari . . .

ANJAN. . . . And if someone wanted to come along with him . . .

SAMIR. Yes, don't worry. We'll definitely send him tomorrow.

SREELA'S GRANDFATHER. That's a very good idea. (*To Haran*) You'd better spend the night here.

Cut to Haran, still squatting on his haunches by the door. He looks at the floor.

HARAN. What should I do? I'm so confused. Oh God, why did this happen to me?

Haran clutches the door, as if for support, and starts crying. Cut to Anjan, Samir and Sreela's grandfather, their heads bent. After a few moments, Sreela's grandfather walks out of the room.

Cut to the balcony, where Sreela's grandfather is standing.

SREELA'S GRANDFATHER. Anjan, please come here. You too, Samir.

Anjan and Samir emerge from the sitting room, and join him on the balcony. The three men start walking towards the staircase.

> SREELA'S GRANDFATHER. Leave him alone for a little while. Let him weep; he'll feel the better for it . . . By the way, I don't see your father anywhere, Samir.
>
> SAMIR. He wasn't feeling too well. He's gone to bed.
>
> SREELA'S GRANDFATHER. Hmmm . . . Sreela, let's make a move, dear.

Low angle shot of the stair landing. The three men stop there and carry on chatting.

> SREELA (*off-screen*). Yes; 'bye, Boudi.
>
> SREELA'S GRANDFATHER. By the way, where will he sleep tonight?
>
> ANJAN. We'll think of something.
>
> SREELA'S GRANDFATHER. He could spend the night at our place.
>
> SAMIR. He could even sleep upstairs, for tonight.
>
> ANJAN. Don't worry, we'll organize something.
>
> SREELA'S GRANDFATHER. All right, then . . .

Sreela, her grandfather and Anjan go down the stairs, while Samir goes upstairs. Mamata is left alone on the empty landing. A few moments later, Mrs Lahiri comes out of the bedroom, goes up the stairs. She climbs a few steps, pauses, then turns around.

> MRS LAHIRI. I'd better get dinner ready . . . By the way, he can eat anything . . . Palan's father, I mean. There're no restrictions till the funeral.

Cut to the stairs. Anjan is seen in high angle shot, coming up the stairs. As he reaches the landing, Mamata can be seen standing there.

> ANJAN. I was thinking . . . he could sleep in the living room for the night . . .

Anjan stops in mid-sentence and looks down the balcony. Mamata looks over her shoulder as well.

Cut to point-of-view shot of Haran standing at the sitting room door, looking at them. Haran slowly walks off towards the kitchen.

Cut to Anjan and Mamata. They walk very slowly upto the sitting room door. Both look embarrassed as well as guilty. Anjan suddenly walks into the sitting room in a rather decisive manner.

Cut to sitting room doorway, from the inside. Mamata in mid-close-up, standing at the door. The sounds of furniture being moved about can be heard off-screen.

Cut to interior of the sitting room. Anjan is moving the furniture towards the walls, creating some room in the centre.

> ANJAN. . . . That's it then, there's plenty of room now . . . What do you say?

Cut to the door. mid-close-up of Mamata. She slowly moves inside the room, all the while looking at her husband rather disdainfully.

Cut back to Anjan, who stands up and looks at Mamata.

> ANJAN. . . . We'll have to spread something on the floor . . . a blanket . . .

Anjan looks at Mamata enquiringly. She remains where she was, and does not answer him. Anjan carries on with his plan to make a bed.

> ANJAN. . . . And he can sleep with his head on this side . . . what we need's a blanket . . . do we have a spare . . . ?

Cut to a silent Mamata, who looks at him almost in disgust.

Cut to the stairs, as Hari comes down in mid-shot. Camera follows him as he crosses the balcony to stand outside the sitting room door. The camera pans right, showing Mamata standing just inside the door. She turns and looks over her shoulder at Hari.

HARI. Boudi, Madam sent this.

Cut to Anjan, who quickly comes up to Hari.

ANJAN. What is it? A blanket? Good, good . . .

MAMATA (*to Hari*). Thanks. Now run along.

ANJAN. Now, if only we had something to lie on . . .

Mamata looks at Anjan in disgust, then leaves.

Cut to the bedroom; Mamata enters the bedroom and sits on the bed, then looks down towards the sleeping Pupai.

Cut to mid-close-up of the sleeping Pupai.

Cut back to Mamata; she lifts the corner of the mattress up and peers underneath. Another, thinner mattress can be seen.

MAMATA. Listen, can you come in here a minute?

Mamata walks back to the bed, as Anjan enters the room behind her. He joins her at the bed, where she has started pulling at the bed sheets.

ANJAN. What is it?

MAMATA. Pick Pupai up, will you? I'll pull this mattress out.

ANJAN. Mattress?

MAMATA. Yes.

ANJAN. You mean that we had a spare one all along and didn't give it to him?

Mamata looks at Anjan for a second, before returning to her job.

MAMATA. Just pick him up, will you?

Anjan reaches over and picks Pupai up and holds him.

ANJAN. Pupai . . . Pupai . . .

MAMATA. There's no need to wake him.

ANJAN (*off-screen*). He's already awake.

PUPAI. What're you doing, Mummy?

MAMATA. Working, love.

Mamata has by now managed to roll the upper mattress two-thirds of the way up towards the top of the bed. She is obviously having great difficulty completing the rest of the task; she lacks the strength for it. Anjan is standing by the side, holding the child and shouting encouragement.

ANJAN. Pull harder . . . harder . . .

Anjan puts Pupai down, goes to the other side of the bed and starts yanking away.

ANJAN (*to Pupai*). Just stand there . . . (*to Mamata*) . . . Now, lift it up . . . lift it up . . . push harder . . . push . . . push . . . push harder . . . harder . . .

Cut to Mamata, pushing harder.

MAMATA. I can't . . . !

ANJAN. Push harder . . . now . . .

The mattress comes free very suddenly in Anjan's hands. Mamata collapses on the other side of the bed, and for the first time, bursts into uncontrollable sobs. The camera slowly tracks across the room till it reaches the door. A low angle shot of Hari, seen through the door. He, too, is watching, his face stony and cold.

Cut to sitting room. Anjan can be seen in mid-shot, standing at the door. Through the sitting room window, Haran can be seen walking towards the sitting room.

ANJAN. Haran, come here, will you . . . It's very late.

Haran comes up to the door next to Anjan, and stares downwards.

Cut to point-of-view shot of a very neatly made bed on the floor of the sitting room.

Cut back to Anjan and Haran.

ANJAN. You can sleep here . . . yes, here . . . if you need the light, the switch is here . . .

Anjan reaches across to the switchboard, and switches the light off and then switches it on again. The entire room is plunged in darkness for a second, then lit up once more. Haran has a look of utter disbelief on his face at all this.

HARAN. But my son . . . the kitchen . . . I'd better stay in that room.

He shakes his head and walks off slowly towards the kitchen. Anjan clenches his jaw in chagrin. Mamata looks at her husband with an outraged expression on her face.

Cut to outside of the police station in long shot. It is morning. A black Maria van is standing outside the building; a police inspector is seen clambering up beside the driver's seat. The van drives off, screen left. As the van departs, Anjan, Haran, Hari and another two men come in from screen left, walk across, and enter the building. Anjan ushers Haran in; Hari and the other men follow. They walk down a corridor, finally coming to a waiting area. Anjan points everyone to a vacant bench.

ANJAN. Wait here, all of you. Hari, look after Haran.

Cut to close-up of Haran's anguished face. Anjan walks past a maze of rooms, before pausing outside one.

Cut to Anjan standing at the door of the room, seen from inside.

ANJAN. May I come in?

INSPECTOR (*off-screen*). Please come in . . . sit down . . .

Camera pans to show the Inspector at his desk, busily writing something. He looks up at Anjan briefly, then goes back to his writing.

INSPECTOR. I'll be with you in a minute.

Cut to Haran and the others, proceeding to sit on a bench.

HARAN (*gesturing to the others*). Sit down.

They watch as a policeman passes by.

Cut to Haran, looking sideways, in the direction Anjan went. The Inspector finishes, and looks up at Anjan. Anjan is facing the Inspector, with his back to the camera.

INSPECTOR. You can take the body.

ANJAN. I can?

INSPECTOR. Yes, I'll give you the disposal slip; all you have to do is go to the morgue.

ANJAN. If you could tell me the address of the morgue . . .

INSPECTOR. Oh, someone'll accompany you, and identify the body for you. But what about the relatives? Have you managed to get hold of any of them?

ANJAN. Oh yes, shall I bring them in?

INSPECTOR. Whom?

ANJAN. Well, the father arrived last night itself. This morning we sent for the brother, and someone from the village.

INSPECTOR. You're certainly not taking any chances, are you? Well, let's hope that they don't cause any problems. One never knows these days . . . You might as well call them in.

ANJAN. All of them?

INSPECTOR. Lord, no! Just the father will do.

Anjan leaves the office. As he leaves the frame, the telephone rings and the Inspector picks it up.

INSPECTOR. Hello . . . yes . . . speaking . . .

Cut to Anjan standing with Haran and the others. He beckons to Haran.

ANJAN. Come with me.

The other three get up as well. Anjan motions them back.

ANJAN (*to Haran*). No, not them. Just you alone.

HARAN. Sir, they've come all this way to look at him once, for
the last time . . .

ANJAN. He's not here . . .

HARAN. Not here . . . ?

Haran looks absolutely astonished at this. Anjan is obviously
embarrassed.

ANJAN. No, we've got to take a letter . . .

HARAN. A letter . . . ?

Anjan is further embarrassed at this. He refuses to look at Haran.
He places his hand on Haran's shoulder.

ANJAN. Yes, come along.

Anjan and Haran walk towards the office. As they leave the frame,
screen right, the camera rapidly moves over the other three people's
faces, before coming to rest on Hari's in close-up. He is looking at
the departing Haran and Anjan.

Cut to close-up of Haran. Camera pulls back to show him in the
Inspector's office. He is fairly overawed and comes forward in a
hesitant manner. He comes up to the Inspector's desk, and greets
him with a namaskar and deep bow, almost an obeisance.

INSPECTOR. Name . . . ? . . . Name?

Anjan sits down. Haran is next to him.

ANJAN. Go on. Tell him.

HARAN. Er . . . Palan, sir.

ANJAN. No, no. He's asking for your name.

HARAN. Haran Chandra Das, sir.

INSPECTOR. Village?

HARAN. Sukharia.

INSPECTOR. Thana?

HARAN. Balagarh.

INSPECTOR. What was that name that you mentioned? Palan.
Your son, was he?

HARAN. My youngest, sir . . .

Haran slowly shakes his head and starts to squat on the floor.

HARAN. I'd sent him to this Babu with great hopes, but my fate!

Haran squats on the floor and slowly shakes his head. The camera remains at standing height; high angle shot of Anjan sitting at the desk, his head down, Haran squatting on his haunches on the floor, with only the head and shoulders showing and the rest obscured by the desk. Haran is still shaking his head. Meanwhile, the Inspector is busily writing something on a form, which he hands to Anjan after he finishes writing.

INSPECTOR. Here we are . . . just show them this . . . I shouldn't
go overboard . . . just get a hearse from the Satkar Samiti.
Shouldn't cost you more than fifty rupees or so.

ANJAN. By the way, what about that post-mortem report?

Haran stands up in shock at the question.

Cut to close-up of a man pulling something, presumably a sliding drawer, open. It opens with a metallic screech.

Cut to Anjan looking downwards, holding a handkerchief in his right hand. He widens his eyes in shock, and quickly covers his face with the handkerchief.

Cut. A young man in his very early thirties comes around the corner of a building, followed by a group of boys ranging from thirteen to seventeen. The camera pans to follow them and reveals Haran and the others squatting on the road, in front of the gate.

YOUNG MAN. There they are; come on.

The young man approaches Haran, who looks up at him in recognition.

HARAN. Oh, Ganesh! Sit, sit. When did you find out?

Ganesh sits next to Haran. The group of boys remains standing. They are all looking very grave.

GANESH. I didn't know anything. I was at my office and was told that my ex-employer was looking for me. They told me everything.

HARAN. What a thing to happen, Ganesh. I still can't . . . Palan!

GANESH (*to kids*). Sit down, all of you.

HARAN. Who're they?

GANESH. They're servants from the neighbourhood, all Palan's friends. They all came running as soon as they saw me and said 'We'll go with you'.

HARAN. You've come to see him? So have we.

Cut to the front of the building. Anjan comes out, followed by two stretcher bearers, carrying a body on a stretcher. The body is totally wrapped in a shroud. Everyone stands up and watches; the camera zooms in on Haran's face.

Cut to point-of-view shot of the body being loaded on to the back of a small pick-up truck, which is parked in front of the building. This shabby vehicle serves as a hearse. The two men lay the body on the back of the truck and raise the back flap. The legend Hindu Satkar Samiti, written in Bengali script, is now visible. Anjan oversees the operation, waits until the truck drives off, then turns and walks back towards the waiting group. He stops when he is opposite Haran, who is looking at the departing truck.

HARAN. He's gone.

ANJAN. Yes. Come on.

HARAN. But where?

Anjan averts his face and raises his arm in a hailing motion.

ANJAN. Taxi . . .

A montage of three shots, progressively revealing more of one particular piece of graffiti. The first shot shows 'Revenge', the next 'We'll take revenge, Samiran', and the last 'We'll take revenge, Samiran, for your death'.

Cut to a large fire burning against the backdrop of a wall covered with graffiti.

Cut to a wall with an advertisement painted on it, announcing Kali Puja, as well as the location of the burning ghat, Nimtala. The camera moves back, to reveal Haran, Ganesh and others sitting around the fire.

Cut to Ganesh in mid-shot, sitting in front of a wall; the graffiti behind him reads 'We won't forget you, Bipul'. Camera pulls back to show the entire group of mourners huddled around the fire, at various distances. Camera pans left, to close-up of Anjan. He is gnawing his lip, and looking into the distance.

Cut to Samir and Sreela's grandfather entering the area from a gate, screen right. They look around, searchingly.

Cut to Ganesh, looking in their direction.

SAMIR. There he is . . .

Cut to Ganesh, with his back to the camera.

Cut to Haran.

The two men walk up to Anjan.

SAMIR (*off-screen*). You haven't had any problems, have you Anjan?

Cut to the sitting Haran. He looks up at the question, then turns his face away. Anjan silently looks over his shoulder at Samir.

Cut to the group huddled around the fire.

SREELA'S GRANDFATHER. What did the post-mortem report say?

ANJAN. Just carbon monoxide poisoning, that's all.

Anjan looks decidedly uncomfortable.

Cut to the group once again, and then to Anjan.

Cut to montage of first wall graffiti, in reverse order. 'We will take revenge for your death, Samiran' . . . 'We will take revenge Samiran' . . . 'Revenge'.

Cut to close-up of Anjan, biting his thumb in a preoccupied manner and looking downwards, screen right.

Cut to Haran sitting by the fire, looking utterly disconsolate.

Cut to Samir, Sreela's grandfather and Anjan. Camera pulls back to reveal Haran and Ganesh in the foreground, sitting together.

SREELA'S GRANDFATHER. Ganesh, come here a minute . . .

Ganesh stands up and approaches Sreela's grandfather. The two of them walk away from the others.

SREELA'S GRANDFATHER. Now that you're here, take care of things, will you. We'll be leaving now.

Sreela's grandfather turns and walks away, leaving the frame screen left. Ganesh is left on his own in the frame for a few moments, staring after them.

Cut to high angle shot of Samir and Sreela's grandfather leaving, followed by Anjan. He pauses about halfway, turns and looks at the mourners. Haran looks up at him for a second, then turns away once again. Camera slowly pans over the faces of the lads sitting by the blaze. All are sombre. Hari has tears on his face. Ganesh arrives from screen left, looking at the departing trio all the while. He finally sits next to Haran, completing the circle around the fire.

Cut to Haran and Ganesh. Ganesh's face looks faintly tear-stained in the ruddy light of the fire.

129

GANESH. Move away from the fire, boys . . . the heat . . .

HARAN. Palan isn't feeling the cold any more . . . !

GANESH. What . . .

Ganesh breaks into soft sobs. Haran looks anguished.

Cut to close-up of two hands, the left holding a bundle of burning twigs and the right a brass tray containing various foodstuffs. The hands approach a man, the lower half of whose body only can be seen. The camera pulls back, to show Mrs Lahiri standing in front of Anjan and Samir.

MRS LAHIRI. Hold your hands over the fire, then touch your chest.

ANJAN. What's all this about?

MRS LAHIRI. You must observe these rituals . . . Now touch the iron bangle. These aren't mere superstitions, you know, these are our traditions. Now, bite the neem leaf and eat a sweet; now cross the threshold . . . you too, Samir; touch the bangle, bite the leaf and take a piece of sweet. Now, come in.

Mrs Lahiri puts out the fire and turns, walking towards the two men.

MRS LAHIRI. . . . There's been a death in the house. You people have returned from the burning ghat. These things are necessary for the well being of the household. (*To Samir*) Close the door. (*To Mamata*) It's too cold for a ritual bath. Tell them to change before entering.

Mrs Lahiri goes up the stairs. Anjan passes Mamata on his way up.

MAMATA. Haven't they come back?

ANJAN. No, they're still at the burning ghat.

Cut to the close-up of a roaring blaze. The camera tilts upwards to show the flames reaching high, and the sparks flying upwards against a black sky.

Cut to the interior of the Sens' bedroom. The camera slowly pans right, revealing Anjan and Mamata lying in bed, with a sleeping Pupai between them. It is clear that a strained distance has grown between husband and wife. Anjan is lying on his back smoking, and staring into nothingness. He seems quite oblivious to every-one's presence. Mamata looks at her husband once, then turns on her side. Her back is now to him. Anjan puts out the cigarette. The sound of someone knocking loudly can be heard off-screen. The sound continues for a little while, before Mamata throws off the blanket and rises.

MAMATA. Can you hear that?

Mamata walks to the bedroom door and opens it, reluctantly fol-lowed by Anjan. They step out onto the landing. Mrs Lahiri can be seen hurrying down the stairs, with Samir in front of her.

MRS LAHIRI. Couldn't you people hear that?

Mrs Lahiri and Samir hurry down the stairs. Anjan and Mamata do not go beyond the landing; they peer down towards the front door.

Cut to Samir opening the front door. Ganesh is standing at the door, with Haran and the boys behind him.

Cut to Samir.

Cut to Ganesh.

Cut to Mrs Lahiri.

Cut back to Ganesh.

GANESH. We're mourners, back from the burning ghat.

Cut to reverse shot. Samir is standing at the door, with Mrs Lahiri visible in the background.

SAMIR. Yes, of course. Come in.

Mrs Lahiri climbs upstairs.

Cut to the Lahiri's bedroom. Benoy is sitting up in bed. Mrs Lahiri enters, and starts rummaging under the bed.

BENOY. Who is it now?

MRS LAHIRI. Palan's father.

BENOY. This late at night?

MRS LAHIRI (*from under the bed*). They've just returned from the burning ghat . . . thank God that these things are all still here . . . Where's the pitcher? . . . As if all the responsibilities are mine . . .

Mrs Lahiri finds the various objects required for the ritual and hurries downstairs again. She walks past Mr Lahiri, then passes Anjan and Mamata on her way down. She comes up to the door, walking past Samir in the process.

MRS LAHIRI. Light it, Samir.

Cut to reverse shot, with the whole group still at the doorstep. Samir lights the twigs and walks away, screen right.

Cut to shot of the door. Ganesh beckons Haran to be the first to enter. Haran goes through the ritual, and enters the house.

Cut to Mrs Lahiri, with a tender expression on her face.

Cut to Samir.

Cut to a little boy doing the ritual and then coming to stand before Haran.

Cut to Haran, looking at Hari.

Cut to Mrs Lahiri.

Cut to pair of feet at the door.

Cut to Ganesh doing the ritual. Haran looks around, as though fixing everything in his memory. The others come in one by one.

Cut to Anjan looking down at them.

Cut to Haran, who walks to the stairs and looks up at Anjan and Mamata, who are standing at the landing. He slowly starts climbing the stairs.

Cut to Samir.

Cut to Ganesh, who is completing the ritual.

Cut to Mrs Lahiri. Ganesh looks up at Haran climbing the stairs and hurries off towards the staircase.

Cut to Haran as he approaches Anjan up the stairs. There is considerable tension in the air. The look on Haran's face is enigmatic. Anjan seems ready to accept whatever befalls him. Mamata's face looks taut with fear and expectation. Pupai emerges and stands next to the curtained door. Haran comes up to Anjan, looks at him gravely for a moment, and does a namaskar. He turns and does the same to Mamata, and finally to Pupai.

HARAN. Goodbye, sir . . . goodbye, ma . . . Khoka babu . . .

Loud music as camera zooms in on Pupai.

Haran turns and slowly walks down the stairs. As he reaches the bottom landing, the camera pans to show the little cubby hole at the bottom of the stairs. The walls are plastered with pictures, including the famous shot of Bruce Lee. The ceiling of the little space seems to press down.

Cut as Haran approaches Hari. He gently caresses Hari's head and face and walks towards the others.

HARAN. Come, Ganesh.

High angle shot from the top of the stairs. They file out one by one. Haran is the last to leave. He reaches the door, turns, and bows. Fade to black.

Suddenly, One Day

Ekdin Achanak (1988)

Translated from the Hindi
Based on a Story by Ramapada Chowdhury

Credits

Script and Direction	Mrinal Sen
Photography	K. K. Mahajan
Sound	B. K. Chaturvedi and Anup Mukherjee
Decor	Gautam Bose
Music	Jyotishka Dasgupta
Editing	Mrinmoy Chakraborty
Executive Producers	Ravi Malik and Debashis Mujumdar (NFDC)
Produced by	National Film Development Corporation (NFDC) and Doordarshan

Cast

Artistes	*Characters*
Sreeram Lagoo	Sasank
Uttara Baokar	Sudha
Shabana Azmi	Neeta
Aparna Sen	Aparna
Roopa Ganguly	Seema
Arjun Chakraborty	Amu
Manohar Singh	Samar
Anil Chatterjee	Arun
Anjan Dutt	Alok
	and others

35 mm/1:1.66/105 min/Eastmancolor/

136

A montage of black-and-white snapshots of a flooded and rain-sodden Calcutta. In the background can be heard the sound of water flowing and of vehicles making their way through water. The first snapshot is of a bus ploughing its way through water, raising a huge wave in front of it. The second, a high angle shot of a flooded street. The camera slowly tilts across the shot, to show a group of people waiting on the pavement. The third, a woman holding a large bag high up, wading through nearly hip-deep water. The fourth, mid-close-up of a car submerged virtually upto the bonnet. The fifth, a close-up of three men pushing a stranded car, taken from the back. The sixth, a mid-long shot of two youngsters floating on a rubber tyre in a flooded street. The seventh, a high angle shot of a long line of people, all with open umbrellas, standing on one side of a flooded street, but facing in the direction of the opposite pavement. The eighth, a school boy wading through a flooded street holding his shoes in one hand, whilst a bus passes beside him. The ninth, a close-up of a bus loaded with people, with passengers spilling out of both doors, making its way through a flooded street. The tenth, people wading through water towards a bus. The eleventh, a long shot of a flooded and deserted road, with a man in a check shirt in the foreground, with his back to the camera, looking down the road. The twelfth, a high angle shot of a traffic jam in a flooded street, with a tram in the right foreground. Montage ends.

mid-close-up of Neeta sitting sideways on a chair, resting her arms and head against the back of the chair.

Cut to Amu lying in bed. He is seen through the bars of a window.

Cut to close-up of Sudha, sitting on a chair.

Cut to Seema in mid-long shot, sitting at a desk, obviously studying, in a room which is only illuminated by the light on the table. She, too, is seen through the bars of a window. The sound of an approaching car suddenly breaks the stillness. A car horn can be heard tooting. All four are immediately attracted to the sound, turning their heads; they all rush out of the room.

Cut to low angle shot of the balcony, with all four coming to look downwards anxiously. The frame freezes.

The credits start rolling, beginning with EKDIN ACHANAK. The frame unfreezes after the credits are over. The camera slowly tracks across the length of the balcony. All the four are looking downwards, out of the frame, towards the unseen car. It drives on without stopping, all of them turning to watch it go by. They leave the balcony one by one, disappointment on their faces, with Seema lingering on.

Cut to mid-shot of Neeta entering the room. She stops near the chair and looks down, then takes a few steps forward, passes the window and stands near the door.

Cut to Sudha and Amu. Amu is lying on the bed, and staring up at the ceiling. Sudha comes and sits beside but facing away from him.

Cut to Neeta, who crosses screen right to left in front of the window, then sits on a chair facing away from both Amu and Sudha.

SUDHA: Seema . . . Amu . . . Neeta, you'd better eat. After all, how long can you wait?

NEETA: What's the hurry? (*Looks back at Sudha.*) We can't even phone anyone. The wretched phone's been dead for two days.

In the mean time, Seema is seen crossing the open window in the background, screen left to right.

AMU: Have you noticed the rain? More than half the telephones in the city must be in the same state.

Neeta rises and leaves the room. Amu turns and lies with his back to Sudha.

Cut to mid-shot of Neeta as she enters the next room through a curtained door, screen left. There is a writing desk in the foreground, with a telephone and a writing lamp upon it. Another door on screen right shows part of a room. A sink with a mirror above it, and a towel rack beside it can be seen. The wall next to this door is covered with a metal book rack, which is full of books. Between the two doors is a small table, with a stack of files upon it. Neeta picks up the telephone receiver and impatiently tries to get a line, looks at it in disgust and slams the receiver down. She circles the table to stand in front of it and examines the various objects lying on it. She picks up a pair of spectacles, then lifts a pad and riffles through the pages before putting it down.

Cut to mid-close-up of Neeta examining the spectacles. The phone rings suddenly, again breaking the quiet. Neeta puts the spectacles down and rushes to the phone, to pick it up.

Cut to Amu, Sudha and Seema, who enter the room and listen intently.

NEETA (*frantically*): Hello . . . hello . . . (*louder*) hello . . . ?

SUDHA: Who is it?

NEETA: Hello . . . ?

AMU: Who's speaking?

SEEMA: Baba?

NEETA: Hello . . . I'm afraid I can't hear you . . . Hello . . . listen, your voice . . .

AMU: What happened?

NEETA: We got disconnected.

Neeta puts the telephone down.

SUDHA: Did you hear anyone's voice?

Cut to close-up of Amu who picks up the receiver. Sudha can be seen in the background. Amu listens for a few seconds, taps the cradle a couple of times and then puts the receiver down.

AMU: Now even the dial tone's gone. Damn!

Cut to a montage of shots of lightning flashing against a dark night sky.

Cut to interior of dining room, with Sudha in the foreground, sitting at the dining table. Neeta is in the background, curled up on a chair, between the two doors. Seema is standing near the door screen right. Amu enters the room through the door screen left, and stands by the door.

SEEMA: It's going to rain again. Rain heavily, at that.

SUDHA: I do wish you people would eat.

NEETA: Ma, why did you let him go out? Why didn't you stop him?

SUDHA: Does he ever pay attention to me, that I . . .

Amu comes up to the dining table and sits next to Sudha.

AMU: What was it you said? When did Baba leave?

SUDHA: Just before seven o'clock, I think. He sat all afternoon in the verandah, without even getting up once.

NEETA: But what had happened? Something must've happened, surely!

SUDHA: I don't know. He was looking at the rain as if he'd never seen it before.

SEEMA: You must've said something. Some comment or the other . . .

SUDHA: Here we go again. She keeps repeating the same thing.

NEETA: Wouldn't Ma tell us if there had been something?

SEEMA: Well, this hardly seems the sort of weather when people go out for the sheer fun of it!

Seema tosses her head and walks out of the room, through door screen right.

Cut to close-up of Amu. Neeta can be seen in the background. Amu is scowling at the departing Seema.

AMU: God! Will this girl ever learn to control her tongue?

SUDHA (*off-screen*): He paced up and down for a long while, then flipped through some books. He even wrote something, like he usually does . . .

Cut to mid-close-up of Sudha.

SUDHA: . . . He tried to contact someone over the telephone a couple of times . . . then he returned to the balcony and sat down again. I gave him a cup of tea at around 5 o'clock. He drank it . . .

Cut to mid-close-up of Neeta.

NEETA: Was there anything else? I mean, did he say anything to you?

Cut to mid-close-up of Sudha.

SUDHA: How often in a day does he talk to me?

Cut to mid-close-up of Amu and Neeta.

AMU: As if he tells us an awful lot . . .

NEETA: Seema?

SEEMA (*off-screen, sounding sharp*): What is it?

NEETA: What're you doing there? Come and join us.

Cut to mid-close-up of Sudha.

SUDHA: The rain had stopped for quite a while ... the water had subsided out in the streets, the water had subsided ... Arati had finished the washing-up and left ... and suddenly ...

(Flashback.)

Cut to the balcony. Sasank is shown in mid-shot, rising from the chair and leaning against the parapet, deep in thought. He looks upwards at the sky and then down at the street. He then turns and leaves the balcony.

Cut to interior of bedroom. It is dark and unlit. Sasank is seen in mid-shot, entering the bedroom. The camera slowly pans right to follow him. Sasank crosses the room screen left to right, goes to a clothes rack and picks up a Jawahar jacket. He wears the Jawahar jacket and switches on the light. There is a bed on the left of the door, with a window at the foot of the bed. Next to the window is a clothes rack and beside that another door. The camera pans left following Sasank as he crosses the room. He goes to the dressing table and sits in front of it. He quickly combs his hair, then opens the lefthand drawer of the dressing table and takes out a wallet. Sasank checks the contents of the wallet before putting it inside the pocket of his kurta, and leaving the room.

Cut to a dark unlit study. Sasank enters through the door screen left. Sudha is visible through the door on the right as Sasank switches on the light and then crosses the room, screen left to right. He sits down at his desk, picks up a small diary and puts it inside his jacket pocket. Sasank then rises and tries the phone.

SASANK: Listen . . .

Sudha comes up to the doorway.

SUDHA: What is it? . . . It's useless trying . . .

Sasank puts the receiver down. The camera pans left as Sasank crosses the room. Sudha is still at the doorway.

SASANK: I'm going out for a while.

SUDHA: But where to?

SASANK: I'll be back in a minute.

Cut to a pair of well-shined shoes. Close-up of Sasank's feet as he wears the shoes

SUDHA: Now? In this awful weather?

Cut to mid-close-up of Sasank. Sudha can be seen in the background. Sasank is picking up his umbrella.

SUDHA: . . . Whoever goes out in this dreadful weather?

SASANK: Everyone else is sitting at home, is it?

SUDHA: But whatever are you going out for?

SASANK: Why? Aren't your children out? Why can't I go out?

Sasank leaves the frame screen left. Sudha is left staring at his retreating back.

(Flashback ends.)

Cut to mid-close-up of Amu at dining table.

AMU: As if the 'children' don't have any business going out. Doesn't Didi have to go to office? To say nothing of my running from pillar to post, going crazy trying to convince people . . . and Seema has her college. As if all these things are nothing at all!

Cut to mid-close-up of Sudha. She is sitting at the dining table as well.

SUDHA: Well, who's to explain it to him? He just sits in his room all day and broods . . . Oh, I don't know . . .

Camera moves a fraction to show Seema entering. She joins the others at the table.

SEEMA: What d'you mean you don't know? Nobody forced him to sit at home, did they? He's lost interest in teaching; he says so himself.

SUDHA: Yes. And look at some of his older colleagues. They've had their jobs extended by five to six years, and still don't want to retire. They just keep on teaching . . .

Neeta's face has been growing increasingly stormy as this conversation carries on. She seems almost near to tears.

NEETA: They keep on teaching and Baba doesn't, is that right? . . . The things you say . . .

Neeta rises and rushes off towards the door, screen right. She pauses at the door and turns towards the others. Only Seema can be seen, however, sitting screen right. Neeta looks as though she is suppressing her tears with the greatest difficulty.

NEETA: Is Baba the sort that sits idle, really? Don't you notice how he pores over his books all day?

The sound of the telephone ringing in the background helps to break the tension. All four rush out of the room, towards screen left.

Cut to the interior of the study. Seema is the first to reach the phone. She picks up the receiver, while the others crowd around and listen intently.

SEEMA: Hello . . . yes . . . yes . . . yes . . .

NEETA: Can you hear anything?

SEEMA: Who is this? Yes . . . This is Seema . . . Who? Oh, it's you. (*To the others*) It's Aparnadi . . . (*To Aparna*) Is something wrong? You're ringing this late? (*To Amu*) What's the time?

AMU: It's ten to midnight.

Sudha takes the phone from Seema.

SUDHA: Hello, hello Aparna. Is everything all right?

NEETA (*to Sudha*): Is Baba there . . . ?

Sudha shakes her head.

SUDHA (*to Aparna*): I see. You want to speak to him? But he's . . .

Cut to close-up of Amu and Seema.

AMU: He's asleep . . . Just tell her he's asleep. Tell her . . .

Cut to Sudha and Neeta in close-up.

SUDHA: Hello . . . he's fast asleep, I'm afraid . . . no, no, just feeling a bit unwell. Was it something important? Yes . . . ?

Cut to mid-close-up of Aparna, sitting at her desk. The room is considerably better furnished and more elegant than Sasank's sitting room. It is also much better decorated. Aparna herself is a smart and elegant young woman, in keeping with her surroundings.

APARNA: No, no let him sleep, it's okay. There's no need to disturb him, it wasn't anything important.

Cut to close-up of Sudha. Neeta enters frame, stands for a while behind Sudha and then sits down.

SUDHA: Hello . . . yes . . . yes . . . yes, yes . . . go on, I'm listening. What? A photograph? What photograph? Who? At our home?

APARNA: Oh, honestly, you forget everything, don't you? We took the photographs that day; Sir was being very difficult, remember? . . . Well, the prints have arrived and they're good, very good indeed. You're there in some of them yourself . . . yes, I'll bring them across one of these days . . . 'bye.

Aparna puts her phone down.

145

Cut to mid-shot of Sudha and Neeta. Sudha puts the phone down and leaves frame. Amu enters screen left, picks up the telephone and stares at it. Neeta is sitting at the desk.

> SUDHA (*to Amu*): Why did you tell me to say that he was asleep?
>
> AMU: What's the point . . . ? Dozens of questions, dozens of explanations . . . (*He picks up the phone and turns to Neeta.*) The phone's working . . . whom should I ring?
>
> NEETA: Uncle Arun, I should think. He's the one friend that . . .
>
> AMU: What's his phone number again?
>
> NEETA: 3 7 . . . er . . . Where's Baba's small diary gone? Where is it? . . . It used to be here . . .

Sudha enters screen left along with Seema. Both start searching for the missing diary all over the room. Meanwhile Neeta is looking through the desk. Seema starts looking through the telephone directory.

> NEETA: . . . Ma, did Baba take it with him, d'you think?
>
> SUDHA: It's possible, I suppose.
>
> NEETA: Well, it's certainly not here.
>
> AMU: Come on, Seema!
>
> SEEMA: 37-7200
>
> AMU: 3 . . . 7 . . . 7 . . . 2 . . . 0 . . . 0. It's ringing, at least. Perhaps he's asleep.
>
> NEETA: If he's asleep, wake him up.
>
> AMU: Hello . . . hello . . . yes, Uncle Arun? This is Amu . . . Amu . . . Amit . . . yes . . . yes . . . no . . . I'm Sasank Ray's son Amit . . . I'm ringing from home.

Cut to Arun. He is sitting at a small telephone table, looking half asleep. Very little can be seen of the room, but what little is visible suggests that he is better off than Sasank.

> ARUN: Yes, yes . . . go ahead. Is something wrong? Why're you ringing so late at night? Good Lord! What're you saying? But when did he leave? What, on such a stormy night? No

...no... he'd not said anything about coming here... in any case, how on earth would he come, in such rotten weather? Yes, it's stopped raining; yes, the water's subsided.

FEMALE VOICE (*off-screen*): What's the matter?

ARUN (*to wife*): Sasank hasn't returned home yet. (*To Amu*) Listen, has he rung you?

Cut to Amu on the phone. The others are gathered around him, listening intently.

AMU: Not yet, no... we're inclined to wait a little while longer ... perhaps by the morning. Yes... perhaps he's got stuck somewhere because of the rain. Yes, yes... Goodbye then ... oh yes, certainly I will.

Amu puts the phone down and turns to Sudha.

AMU: He suggested reporting it to the police.

SUDHA: The police? What for?

SEEMA: Isn't that what everyone will suggest—the police, hospitals and so on?

SUDHA: Listen Neeta, perhaps he's trying to reach us, but can't get through. I mean it's possible, isn't it?

Neeta picks up the phone, and starts dialling.

SEEMA: Now who're you ringing?

NEETA: Mamaji.

SEEMA: Mamaji? He's hardly likely to go there.

SUDHA: No, let her ring. He has a tremendous number of contacts. There's hardly anyone important he doesn't know ... and he's family.

Cut to close-up of Seema, looking at the floor.

Cut to point-of-view shot of a piece of paper lying on the floor, near Sudha's saree.

Cut; the camera slowly draws back to show Seema's hand picking up the piece of paper.

Cut, as the camera tilts up to a close-up of Seema's face, as she examines the paper.

SEEMA (*looking up*): Didi!!

Cut to low angle shot of all four looking down. None of them, however, is willing to meet the other's eye. Their gaze is on the piece of paper and Sasank's voice is heard off-screen.

SASANK: I don't know what the matter is today. Nothing feels right. Nothing at all feels right.

They all exchange glances.

Cut to a busy Calcutta street. The camera tracks down the length of the street, against the flow of traffic. Cars, buses, trucks, minibuses and omnibuses, all flash past, to the accompaniment of a cacophonic din. The pavements are bustling with pedestrians.

Cut to the dining room. The round dining table has a white table cloth covering it. Sudha is in the foreground, centre screen. Opposite her is a grey-haired man in a dark jacket and tie; next to him is a woman. Neeta is standing at the background left. Amu enters through door right, opens the refrigerator, takes out a bottle of water and starts drinking from it.

NEETA: Mamaji, can I get you a cup of tea?
SAMAR: Only if all of you're having some.

Neeta lightly touches his shoulder and leaves the room, passing Seema, who is standing near the sink. Neeta reaches the kitchen door.

NEETA: Arati!

Cut to the interior of the kitchen. Arati is seen putting the kettle on.

Cut to the dining room, seen through the door. Sudha and Samar are sitting at the table. The camera follows Samar as he gets up, enters the study and examines the writing pad. Sudha looks on from behind. He puts the pad down and turns around.

SAMAR: He didn't leave a message by any chance, did he? The way he always does?

Cut to Neeta tidying her hair, with Seema standing behind her.

SEEMA: No . . .

Cut to Amu in mid-close-up. He looks up in utter amazement.

Cut to Seema and Neeta. Neeta goes back to the kitchen. The camera pans to show Seema following her.

NEETA: Arati . . .

Cut to Amu. He is leaning against the bars of the open window.

Cut to the girls' bedroom. Neeta is standing against a large chest of drawers. On top of it are a number of items, but in pride of place at the centre is a portrait in brown. Seema enters the room, screen right. Neeta turns to look at her. She seems to be both angry and perplexed. Seema on the other hand, looks defensive.

SEEMA: What is it?
NEETA: Why did you say he hadn't left any messages? The note said quite clearly 'Nothing feels right'.
SEEMA: But Baba's forever writing things. Anyway, if we'd shown them the note all we'd have got would be a hundred questions.

Neeta frowns and leaves the room through the door, screen right. Seema is left, in mid-close-up. She gnaws her lip in chagrin.

Cut to the dining room. Samar joins his wife, Nisha, and Sudha at the dining table.

SAMAR: The very least you could've done was report it to the police . . . You didn't do even that.

Amu comes in from screen left and joins them at the table. Arati enters from screen right, carrying a tray with a number of cups etc. on it.

SAMAR: . . . You didn't even bother to do that . . . It's morning and all of you're just sitting here!!

SUDHA: But we hadn't even considered going to the police.

SAMAR: A man is missing since last evening and doesn't return home!

Neeta enters the room behind Arati, but stands near the door.

AMU: We thought he'd be back by now . . . er, I mean any moment now.

SAMAR: But he isn't, is he!

SEEMA (*off-screen*): But who could imagine that . . .

SAMAR: Well, that's precisely why you should've reported it to the police; without any procrastination. That would've been the appropriate thing to do. What everyone does, as a matter of fact!

NEETA: We thought that he'd return in the morning sometime. That perhaps he'd got stuck somewhere. (*The sound of the doorbell can be heard in the background as Neeta is speaking.*)

Cut; Seema quickly reaches the front door and opens it. A middle aged, bespectacled and grey-haired man is standing outside.

SEEMA: Uncle Arun!

ARUN : Not back yet?

SEEMA: No. Please come in.

Arun enters. Seema closes the door.

Camera follows Arun as he walks towards the dining room.

SAMAR (*smiling*): Please, sit down.

SUDHA: Come and sit here.

ARUN: No, no, please stay where you are. I'm fine here.

AMU (*off-screen*): Why don't you sit here, Ma?

SAMAR: When did you find out . . . ?

ARUN: Last night. (*To Amu*) When was it? Around midnight, wasn't it?

SAMAR: Isn't that about the time you rang us as well?

NEETA: Yes. To begin with we couldn't get through. The phone wasn't working. Then suddenly we got a call, after which I rang you.

SAMAR: A call? From whom?

NEETA: From Aparnadi.

SAMAR: Who?

SUDHA (*off-screen*): She used to be a student of his.

ARUN: She teaches at the same college.

Cut to Sudha and Nisha, sitting side by side at the table.

NISHA: Wasn't it rather late to be phoning someone?

SUDHA: That's the way they are, both of them. No concept of time whatsoever . . . well, I imagine they're doing something, like a project perhaps.

Cut to Arun. He is fiddling with a bunch of keys.

ARUN: Doing something . . . ? Sasank was helping her in connection with some thesis, that's all.

SAMAR: Oh, supervising . . .

ARUN: Not really, not officially. Just casually helping, you know.

Cut to a grave Seema who enters the room and leans against the wall, behind Samar. Arati enters the room through the door behind Samar.

> SAMAR: That's all very well, but you people didn't find it neces-
> sary to inform the police ... because the police'd come here,
> make enquiries, ask questions of the neighbours, people
> would start gossiping, et cetera, et cetera, et cetera ... That's
> it, isn't it?
>
> ARUN (*off-screen*): No, that's not it at all.
>
> SEEMA (*to Arati*): Have you hung out the washing?
>
> ARATI: Yes.
>
> SEEMA: Off you go, then.

Arati leaves the room, followed by Seema. The camera follows the two of them as they leave.

Cut to Samar and Arun, in mid-close-up.

> SAMAR: That woman has to work in at least five houses in order
> to survive. How long d'you think it'll take for the story to
> spread? Whom are you going to hide it from? And for how
> long? In fact, can you keep it a secret at all?

Cut to Amu listening. He looks up and walks out of the room, through door right.

Cut to Amu's room. Amu enters through door right. Next to the door are some clothes, hanging from hooks on the wall. At the far end of the wall is a small wardrobe. Between the two is a cabinet. Amu crosses the room to screen left and goes to a writing table, with a briefcase lying on top of it. He takes a wallet out of the briefcase, checks it cursorily, puts it in his pocket and walks out of the room.

Cut to Amu walking towards the front door. Seema crosses him, going in the opposite direction.

152

SAMAR (*to Amu*): Wait, there's no need for you to go anywhere.

Cut to Amu, in mid-shot. He turns to look back.

Cut to Samar and Arun at the dining table.
SAMAR: Where's the telephone?
Samar gets up and walks to the telephone.

Cut to Samar at the phone. He is seen through the open door right. The others sitting at the table can be seen on his left.
NISHA: You could speak to the Commissioner, surely.
SAMAR: I'm perfectly aware of whom to speak to.

Cut to Seema, who looks exasperated at the way Samar snaps out. She shakes her head and leaves the room, screen right, out of the frame.

Cut back to Samar in mid-shot. He is seen through the open door, still busy on the phone. The others are sitting at the dining table, avoiding one another's eyes. The silence is broken by the sound of the doorbell ringing. Everyone looks up expectantly. Neeta rises, goes towards the door.
NEETA: Who can it be now?
Neeta leaves the frame, towards the front door. Sudha walks halfway down to the door, looking very anxious and agitated. The others are seen behind her, also looking worried.
SUDHA: Who is it? What is it . . . what's the matter?
SEEMA: Has something happened?

Cut to Neeta in mid-close-up, as she closes the door by leaning back against it. She looks troubled and is trying to choke back tears.

NEETA: What would happen? What's wrong with you people? What did you expect had happened? Wouldn't I tell you if something'd happened? D'you really imagine I'd have kept it a secret?

Neeta virtually runs into her room.

Cut to Neeta standing at her table. Slowly she sits down and cries bitterly. She buries her head in her arms and cries.

Cut to an open window with bars. Very little of the outside is seen through the window. The camera moves back slowly, revealing Seema sitting on a chair reading a magazine. The chair is next to Sudha's bed. Sudha is sitting on the bed, with her back resting against the wall. The cawing of crows can be heard in the background. Sudha suddenly sits up with a start.

SEEMA: What is it?

SUDHA: It sounded as though the phone was ringing . . .

Seema looks at Sudha and shakes her head. They look up as they hear a sudden harsh sound.

Cut to Arati cleaning the floor. She is on her hands and knees. Neeta is sitting in front of her dressing table. She gradually rises as she puts on her earrings and bangles, looking sideways.

Cut back to Sudha and Seema. Seema is now idly turning the pages of the magazine. Sudha is looking preoccupied.

SUDHA: . . . It's been so many days now . . . he was writing all the time, night and day . . . at least if he'd written a message before leaving . . . Seema, if you'd only searched his study carefully . . . if we'd searched his study carefully, perhaps—

SEEMA: Oh, Ma! Can't you see? If Baba'd wanted to say something . . . (*A loud clatter can be heard from outside the bedroom.*) . . . Oh for goodness' sake, Arati!

SUDHA: Y'know, that's what your father always said—Arati
makes a lot of noise but does very little.

SEEMA: Yes, well . . .

Cut to the balcony, where Arati can be seen in mid-shot. She is on
her haunches, wiping the floor. Seema appears at the doorway,
looking quite irate.

SEEMA: What's your big hurry, anyway? Aren't you able to do it
a bit more slowly?

Seema goes back to the bedroom. Neeta appears at the door at the
far end of the balcony, carefully avoids stepping over the wet bits
and enters the bedroom.

Cut to the bedroom. Neeta enters, comes up to the bed and sits
on it, then holds her mother's hands.

NEETA: Ma, I'm off to work. Take care of yourself.

Sudha nods faintly. Mother and daughter look at one another,
intently but tenderly, for some moments.

Cut to Arati in mid-shot, standing at the doorway.

ARATI: Should I clean the study, Maji?

SUDHA: No, let it be.

Arati leaves.

Cut to Sudha and Neeta. Neeta is standing with her back to the
camera, speaking to her mother.

NEETA: Why?

SUDHA: It's okay, I'll do it. I'm all alone in the afternoons anyway,
once the three of you've left. What'm I supposed to do with
myself all day?

NEETA: It's getting late, Ma. I'm off.

SUDHA: Alright.

Neeta is about to leave, when Seema appears with an umbrella.

SEEMA (*smiling*): Didi, you forgot your umbrella.

NEETA: Shouldn't you be at college?

SEEMA: I'm going any minute.

Neeta walks towards the front door and Seema is about to enter the bedroom, then turns back, as she hears her name being called.

Cut to the two of them at the doorway of the bedroom.

NEETA: Seema . . . ?

SEEMA: Yes, what is it?

NEETA: Will you be late returning from college?

SEEMA: No, but why d'you ask?

NEETA: Well . . . it's just that Ma's alone.

SEEMA (*smiling*): I'll return early.

Cut to the staircase. A man in his fifties is ascending the stairs. He stops as he reaches Neeta, who is going down.

NEETA (*politely*): Namaste.

NEIGHBOUR: Any news?

NEETA: No.

NEIGHBOUR: No news yet? Why, for God's sake?

NEETA: Now, how can I answer that?

Neeta and the neighbour carry on in their separate directions.

Cut to the flat. Sudha is grim. Seema slams the door shut and turns; she looks very annoyed.

SEEMA: Really, some people don't even know how to speak in a civil manner. It really makes me mad; Baba disappears and everyone acts as though it was entirely our doing.

Sudha at the door, looking at Seema rushing past her.

Cut to a busy street. The camera tracks across the traffic; the sound of someone being hit by a vehicle can be heard off-screen.

Cut to Neeta's office. The sound of a car braking, followed by off-screen sounds indicating that someone has been hurt. Everyone rushes to the windows, eagerly discussing the accident.

1ST PERSON: It's an accident. Look, there . . . it's a traffic accident.

2ND PERSON: Where . . . where . . . ?

3RD PERSON: There . . . look . . .

Cut to a man in his late thirties, who has not left his desk. He is speaking on the phone.

ALOK: Yes . . . Listen, I'll call you back later . . . Yes.

Cut to a low angle shot of the front of the building. People can be seen leaning out of the windows.

Cut to Neeta arranging papers on her table. She is the only other one in the room who is not looking at the accident. Neeta looks very distressed, as voices can be heard off-screen, eagerly discussing this accident and others in gruesome detail.

1ST VOICE: Look . . . look . . .

2ND VOICE: There . . . Oh my God!

3RD VOICE: Where, oh yes . . . yes.

4TH VOICE: It's an old man; he's really smashed up, isn't he?

1ST VOICE: Old lady and her child in our neighbourhood got run over the other day. Smashed into jelly.

Neeta leaves the room in a distressed state. She is on the verge of tears. Alok looks back at Neeta, absolutely disgusted at the goings-on.

ALOK: What's going on here? What's wrong with you people?

The animated discussions continue off-screen.

ALOK: Stop it. Don't you people have any feelings at all?

Cut to Samar's sitting room. This is obviously the house of a very affluent person. It is very elegantly and luxuriously furnished. What can be seen of the other rooms through the various open doors, etc., shows that they are equally smart. Neeta is sitting on an armchair. Samar enters, pats Neeta on her shoulder and sits, screen right. Nisha is sitting opposite Neeta.

SAMAR: No . . . no. Look, it's highly unlikely that he met with an accident or anything like that. At least, the police don't think that he did. They've investigated every possibility for many days now.

NISHA: Before you notice, the days pass by . . .

SAMAR: These people . . . I mean the police, were saying . . . I mean they think . . . well, at least that's what they told me—

NEETA: What?

SAMAR: If it was something else . . . well, what can the police do about it?

NEETA: Something else?

SAMAR: I mean . . . they're saying that if there'd been any quarrels or arguments, or anything like that at home, then . . .

NISHA: Meaning an unpleasantness, a fight. Isn't that right?

NEETA: A quarrel? But who's going to quarrel in our home? And that, too, with Baba! There was no one that he even—

NISHA: All of us know that, love.

NEETA: All Ma keeps repeating is—why didn't he leave a message?

SAMAR: Your mother isn't the only one, you know. This is precisely what the police are saying . . .

Samar gets up and walks away towards the opposite end of the room, away from the two women. He lights a pipe.

SAMAR: . . . How's Amu's business doing?

NEETA: He doesn't tell us anything . . . just keeps to himself . . .

SAMAR: He would've told you, if things had gone right for him.

NEETA: Baba asked him about it a couple of times.

SAMAR: He did? What did the boy say?

Samar turns to face Neeta.

NEETA: Amu doesn't care to be questioned.

SAMAR: Hmmm . . . (*Turns back again.*) Neeta, perhaps you're aware . . . your father . . . I mean, he was very worried about Amu . . . he had such hopes that Amu would work hard at his studies and make a career for himself . . . that he'd . . . he'd make his family proud of him . . . join his father's profession . . . but . . . but he . . .

NISHA (*off-screen*): And presumably Sasank left home, a broken-hearted man, because of this, eh? Really, you do go on sometimes.

SAMAR (*as he turns to stand behind Neeta, though facing the opposite direction*): Sometimes I think . . . I don't know . . . did you people ever feel that . . . that your father, despite living in your midst . . . that he was quite isolated from all of you . . . quite alone . . . ?

Camera slowly zooms to a close-up of Neeta.

(Flashback begins.)

Cut to a dark study. Sasank is sitting at his writing desk. The only light in the room comes from the lamp on the desk, illuminating the table in a small pool of light. Sasank is reading a book by the light of the lamp; he puts the book down, removes his spectacles and covers his face with his hands. He then stretches back on the chair and looks at the ceiling. He shakes his head mildly.

Cut to a point-of-view shot of a fan rotating overhead.

Cut; Neeta enters the room, quietly comes up behind Sasank and puts her hands on his shoulder. He holds her hands and brings her around, in front of him.

SASANK (*smiles gently*): Neeta? Come here, love.

She sits on the table, facing Sasank.

NEETA: How much longer're you going to read for, Baba?

SASANK: Is it late? What time is it?

Cut to a black-faced alarm clock, standing on the mantelpiece. It has only one hand, pointing to ten o'clock. Both father and daughter burst out laughing, after looking at the clock.

NEETA: Honestly, Baba! What's so special about this clock? Every time I remove this clock, you bring it back. What's so special about it, anyway?

Neeta walks across to the clock and removes it, but Sasank promptly stretches his arm out for it.

SASANK: Hey . . . hey, hey, one minute, give that to me.

He takes the clock back from Neeta and immediately starts winding it up.

NEETA: Really!

SASANK: Look, I know it's got one hand instead of two. But it's still working, you know.

NEETA: In that case, tell me, what time is it?

SASANK: Oh I couldn't tell you that. The second hand's missing.

Neeta laughs.

NEETA: Then what's the point . . . ?

SASANK: Nonetheless, it's still going.

NEETA: Only because you're making it go.

SASANK: But it is going. It's alive.

NEETA: And so are we all, all alive.

SASANK: That's it, we're all alive, breathing—but where are we to go?

Neeta walks back to the desk and sits on it. They remain silent for a few moments, lost in their own thoughts. The silence is suddenly broken by the ringing of the telephone. Sasank immediately attempts to pick up the receiver, but is prevented from doing so by Neeta. She has a mischievous grin on her face.

NEETA: Aparnadi . . .

Father and daughter, both laugh. Neeta removes her hand from the telephone. Sasank finally picks up the receiver.

SASANK: Hello . . .

(Flashback ends.)

Cut to the girls' bedroom. Seema is fast asleep. Neeta is lying in bed reading a book. A little bedside lamp next to her provides the only illumination, in an otherwise dark room. Neeta switches the lamp off and attempts to go to sleep. She suddenly rises, however, and leaves the room.

Cut; Neeta walks through a dark corridor.

Cut to a dark study. Neeta enters, switches on a light and looks around.

Cut; point-of-view shot of Sudha, sitting at the desk looking utterly bereft. Neeta goes and sits next to her mother.

NEETA: Ma, what's wrong? Why're you sitting here alone like this? Ma . . . (*Sudha carries on crying soundlessly. Neeta holds her tight and comforts her as though she were a small child.*) Oh Ma, what madness is this? All you'll succeed in doing is to make your life unbearable, by crying like this . . . come on . . . I'll sleep in your room tonight . . .

She slowly leads Sudha out of the study.

Cut; Amu silently appears out of the darkness and stands at the door of the study. He watches his mother and sister, as they leave without noticing him. After they have gone, he enters, quietly switches off the light and leaves.

Cut to Sudha's bedroom. It is daytime. Sudha is sleeping. The harsh cawing of crows is heard in the background. The sound of the phone ringing is suddenly heard off-screen. Sudha wakes with a start and rushes out of the bedroom.

Cut to the study. Sudha appears at the door of the study. The phone stops ringing. Sudha stops at the door for a few moments, then slowly goes to the desk and walks around it, stands beside the chair, with her hands on the table, and looks around the room. After a little while, she stares rather thoughtfully at the various articles on the desk, then looks through a writing pad very carefully. She picks up a clipboard with some papers attached to it. Cut to close-up of scribblings and illustrations on them. She puts it down. Sudha now starts searching the desk for something. She takes out a piece of paper, looks at it briefly and puts it back. She is unable to find whatever it is she is looking for and goes to the bookshelves, which she starts looking through in a frantic manner. Now and then she pulls out some slips of paper from among the books and puts them back. Suddenly a number of books tumble out and along with them, an envelope. Sudha picks up the envelope and looks closely at it; she seems to become more disturbed, the longer she looks at it. She sits on the bed.

Cut to a close-up of the envelope—a long manila envelope which has 'Aparna' written all over it, in a variety of ways. The handwriting is presumably Sasank's.

SUDHA: Aparna . . . ?!

The doorbell rings suddenly. Sudha hurriedly puts the books back on the shelves and hides the envelope amongst the books. She composes herself before going to the front door and opening it. A smiling Aparna is seen standing at the door.

APARNA (*her smile fades as Sudha remains grim*): I'm . . . I'm so sorry I didn't call on you sooner. I just couldn't make it . . .

Sudha remains absolutely silent. Aparna looks quite embarrassed.

APARNA: In any case, what could I have said . . .

Sudha still maintains her stony silence. Aparna is looking visibly uncomfortable by now and seems completely unsure of what to do next.

APARNA: These photographs were with me; I'd have dropped them in, but . . .

SUDHA: Come in.

Sudha turns away.

(Flashback begins.)

Sasank is standing in front of the mirror, shaving. He looks at the camera.

SASANK: Oh! Come in, come in . . . Come inside, come.

Cut to close-up of Aparna. The camera then moves back to show Arun standing behind Aparna. Seema is standing at the doorway.

APARNA: I'm not alone, though.

SEEMA: Uncle Arun . . .

Cut to Sasank at the mirror.

SASANK: Arun, come in, come in. Sit; I'll be with you in a minute.

Arun and Aparna enter the study from screen left, with Seema leading the way.

SEEMA: Please, sit down.

Arun goes and sits behind Sasank's desk. Aparna stands behind him and examines the books on the shelves. Seema moves to screen left and opens a window.

ARUN (*to Aparna*): Sit down, won't you.

APARNA: Hmmm . . . ?

Seema starts dusting, picking up the various journals etc. strewn all over the room and generally straightening the room out.

SASANK (*off-screen, to Aparna*): You just turn up, without even informing me . . .

APARNA: I wanted to surprise you . . . This collection of yours is quite fantastic.

Seema looks up as she is dusting the books. Sasank enters and sits on the chair behind the desk.

SASANK: They're almost all my father's books. I haven't been able to increase the collection by much . . . Have you noticed the indexing? Even that was done by my father.

APARNA: Fabulous!

ARUN: I was his student.

APARNA: Really?

SASANK: Yes, he was . . . Read this. It has my article.

APARNA: Which article? That one . . . ?

ARUN: The one that you were talking about?

SASANK: Yes, that's right. It'll be controversial. Some people'll certainly raise a hue and cry . . . (*To Aparna*) Let it be for now . . . Read it at home. Read it carefully.

ARUN: But we didn't come here together, you know.

APARNA: Yes, as a matter of fact, we met downstairs.

ARUN: I've come on some other work. Today, I'm also going to spring a surprise.

SASANK: Seema! Ask them to make some tea, will you dear.

Seema stops her dusting and leaves the room. Camera follows her to the kitchen.

Cut to the interior of the kitchen. Sudha is washing dishes at the sink. Seema comes and stands beside her.

SEEMA: D'you know her, Ma?

SUDHA: Whom?

SEEMA: The one who just arrived.

SUDHA: She's never been here before.

SEEMA: Very dignified . . . And look at Baba! He didn't even bother to introduce her.

Cut to the corridor, where Neeta can be seen. She is carrying a saree and a blouse on a hanger. She stops and looks towards her mother and sister.

NEETA: Who knows, he might've mistaken you for the maid.

Neeta leaves, enters the bathroom, screen right.

Cut to Seema and Sudha at the kitchen.

SEEMA (*laughs*): Yeah . . .

SASANK (*off-screen*): I say, are you there?

SEEMA: Off you go then, O maid's mum!

Seema leaves the room, laughing.

Cut to Sasank at the desk.

SASANK: Come in for a moment, won't you?

Sudha enters the room somewhat hesitantly. She crosses she room to stand next to Arun, whom she greets with a namaskar.

SUDHA: What is it?

SASANK: It's Arun; he wants to talk to you.

SUDHA: Namaskar.

ARUN: Namaskar, Bhabhi. What I have to say'll require your presence. You're the only one who can . . . make him understand.

Aparna starts trying to draw Sasank's attention to something. In a few moments, everyone starts looking enquiringly at Aparna.

ARUN: What?

Cut to Sasank in mid-close-up. He looks at Aparna enquiringly.

SASANK: What?

APARNA: Lather?

Sasank rubs his left ear.

SASANK: Lather? Has it gone?

Cut to mid-close-up of Aparna. She smiles hugely and shakes her head. Camera now moves back until everyone can be seen, grouped round the desk.

SUDHA: Now you see what he's like. Something's always . . .

SASANK: I'm sorry. This is Sudha, my wife.

APARNA: I'm Aparna.

SUDHA: Hello.

SASANK: Brilliant girl! She was a very brilliant student. She's joined the faculty recently, become a colleague, in fact.

SUDHA: I see.

ARUN: Listen, can I finish what I came to tell you? I'm in a bit of a hurry.

SASANK: You're always dying to leave within minutes of arriving.

Aparna gets up and goes to the far corner of the room, where she starts looking at the books once again.

SUDHA: Not everyone's like you, you know. Some people work.

SASANK: Did you hear that? It's her perennial complaint.

ARUN: I've had a scheme in my head for a long time. Now, I've finally made it a reality. I've opened a 'Tutorial Home'.

SASANK: Oh . . . wonderful.

Cut to mid-close-up of Aparna. She looks up from the book she has been examining in some astonishment, at hearing Sasank's comment.

Cut to mid-close-up of Arun, who is looking earnestly at a disinterested Sasank.

Cut to a composite shot, with a disgusted Sudha and an amused Aparna listening in to the conversation.

ARUN: You'll have to do more than merely congratulate me. I want you to teach there.

SASANK: Teach? Who, me? In a 'Tutorial Home'?

ARUN: Now don't you say no. Bhabhi, you tell him. It's only an hour a day and in the evenings, at that. They're all B.A. students, in their final year.

SASANK: Listen, who's going to do the teaching? Is it me or Bhabhi? What're you convincing her for, eh?

Aparna smiles, tongue-in-cheek.

ARUN: It's not as if you can't spare the time, is it? You're sitting at home all day.

SASANK (*to Sudha*): You liked that bit, didn't you? Sitting at home ... (*To Arun, laughingly*) That's what they all say, sitting at home ...

ARUN: Well, they're not wrong, are they? And anyway, we can all do with some extra money.

SASANK: Look, I've got my pension ... the providend fund money's lying in the bank ... Neeta's working. Amu ... he's alright. Plus, I've got this house as my inheritance. It even fetches me rent, from upstairs and downstairs, however little that may be. I mean to say, I do get some rent.

Cut to Aparna, examining the bookshelves.

ARUN: And so you do, so you do. But prices keep going up ...

SASANK: I don't know anything about that. That's not something that I get involved in. In any case, these people never tell me anything. (*To Sudha*) Well ...? D'you ever tell me anything about such matters? Do you?

ARUN: Well, if you don't make him understand, who will? I've told him so many times to compose a few 'Notes'.

SUDHA (*to Arun*): Do you really imagine that I haven't told him? Or that the children haven't?

Aparna looks up at Sasank.

ARUN: Moreover, it's not as if he's got to write anything new. Everything's already there. (*Arun points to the journals on a shelf.*) It's all in those things over there. Put something from there here, something from here, there, mix'em up into one and behold—your 'Notes'.

Cut to Aparna, laughing.

SASANK: Listen, my dear fellow. Nobody'd touch these so-called 'Notes' of your's that are floating about in the market. They'd all vanish into oblivion if I started writing . . .

SUDHA: Did you hear that? Honestly! (*To Aparna, smilingly*) You tell me.

APARNA: The thing is . . . I don't think Sir's capable of doing something like that.

SASANK: That is true. I think it's beyond me. I proved to be a bad teacher. Bad . . . ! Very bad . . . ! !

Cut to the corridor. Seema emerges in the background, carrying a handbag. Neeta also comes out into the corridor; she is drying her hair with a towel. Neeta is wearing the sari she was carrying earlier. Seema no longer looks her earlier, cheerful self.

SEEMA: Just listen to Baba talk. God, he's so arrogant. The Lord only knows what he thinks of himself.

Seema exits the frame screen left; the camera follows a faintly smiling Neeta to her room, finally focusing on the photograph on the top of the chest of drawers. Slow fade to black.

(Flashback ends.)

Cut to a close-up of Neeta's hands, holding various snapshots of a smiling Sasank. The camera pulls back to show her looking at the pictures. She goes to the door.

NEETA: Ma?

SUDHA: Yes, dear, what is it?

Cut to a shot of Seema, seen through the bars of the window. She is ironing.

SEEMA: What is it, Didi?

Seema puts down the iron.

Cut to Seema, entering the room. She sits next to Neeta on the bed and starts examining the photographs.

NEETA: Photographs of Baba.

SEEMA: Aren't they nice!

NEETA: Look at this one . . .

SEEMA: Where did you find them?

NEETA: In his desk. In the drawer, you know. Look at this one; isn't he looking . . . Oh, look at this one . . . they were in Aparnadi's envelope.

The two sisters are obviously delighted by the pictures of their father. A very serious-looking Sudha comes and joins them.

SUDHA: Aparna came this afternoon. She was meant to drop the pictures by.

NEETA: But these were taken ages ago . . .

SUDHA: Well, she hadn't visited for a long time.

SEEMA (*laughingly*): Look at this one. What a lovely face he's made. So sweet! Dada, come and take a look.

Neeta gets up and sits in a chair, next to Sudha. Sudha, however, remains standing.

NEETA: Yes, she hadn't come to see us for quite some time. Did she say why?

SUDHA (*grimly*): No.

A smiling Amu enters the room through door right and sits next to Seema.

AMU: What is it?

SEEMA: Come on, take a look. Pictures of Baba; the ones Aparnadi took.

AMU: Oh . . . really? (*He comes and sits beside Seema on the bed.*)

SEEMA (*smiles happily as she shows the photographs to Amu*): Isn't he looking cute? And that's you. And look, here's Ma.

NEETA: Here, let me have a look. (*To Sudha*) They're nice. And you didn't tell us about them. You kept them hidden from us . . . Hmmm . . .

Sudha doesn't answer. In fact she remains very serious looking.

SEEMA: Wait. Just let me catch Aparnadi! I'm really going to get cross with her . . . she didn't bother to take even a single picture of mine . . . Oh, look at this one! Isn't it nice?

Seema is examining the snapshots with great enthusiasm. In the meanwhile, however, Amu has become extremely grim. He angrily throws the photographs that he was holding aside, scattering them on the bed.

Cut to mid-close-up of Neeta.

NEETA: Now what's wrong?

Cut to Seema and Amu. Seema seems rather perplexed at Amu's attitude. She picks up a snapshot and shows it to Amu.

AMU: I don't like it. I don't like any of it.

NEETA: What don't you like?

AMU: These . . . these . . . all these pictures.

SEEMA: Why? Aren't they nice?

Amu knocks the pictures away from Seema's hand. They scatter over the bed; Amu rises and stands next to the door. He looks quite angry.

AMU: I don't care who likes them; I don't . . .

Cut to a montage of five snapshots of a smiling Sasank, taken from various angles.

Cut to Amu pacing up and down angrily.

> AMU: Can't you see how happy he looks; as if he's about to burst with joy . . . He's beaming with . . . could anyone imagine, could anyone, that this . . . this . . . that this was a person who'd just leave everything behind and disappear? Did he even for a moment consider what would happen to us? Did he? Just for once? If he'd had the slightest sympathy for us, just the slightest bit, he'd have tried to understand us . . .

Amu stops for a brief moment or two, but keeps pacing up and down.

> NEETA (*off-screen*): What's got into you all of a sudden?
> AMU: Nothing . . .

Amu walks across to the mirror and stands in front of it, musing, before turning and pointing towards Neeta.

> AMU: Today, now, the responsibility for this entire household's landed on your shoulders, Didi.

Cut to a close-up of a snapshot, of a quizzical-looking Sasank.

Cut to a close-up of Neeta, looking rather surprised at Amu's vehemence.

Cut to Amu standing in front of the mirror, stooping down a bit in order to rest his arms on the top of the dressing table. His image can be seen in the mirror, but he himself is looking away from it.

> AMU: I mean, what do I give you, what help am I, anyway! Occasionally I make a bit of money; when I do, I give you some. At other times, I don't . . . these tenants . . . they've been here for the last twenty-seven years . . . how much do we get from them . . . ?

Sudha has been standing behind Neeta. She goes to the bed and starts picking up the photographs. Neeta joins her.

SUDHA: Amu, your father never ran the household out of the rent he received.

AMU (*off-screen*): That's fine, Ma . . . You think Baba's money's lying in the bank, don't you? So it is. But it'll rot there, I tell you; the money's going to rot there. That money's not your money, nor mine, nor Didi's, nor even Seema's. That money doesn't belong to any of us. That's Baba's money. You've got a cheque book, haven't you? Well, you can keep it; but the money is Baba's . . .

Cut to Amu in close-up. The camera pulls back slightly, to show him standing in front of the mirror. He looks very, very angry.

AMU: . . . I didn't tell you people, but I went to the bank. That money'll stay in the bank for seven years; for seven whole years. That is, if Baba doesn't return in seven years . . .

Cut to Sudha and Neeta, who are both looking stunned.

AMU: . . . And these were the bank manager's words, not mine.

NEETA (*turns angrily towards Amu*): Amu, that's enough! Just stop it now.

Cut to Amu, still standing in front of the dressing table. He seems quite spent after his tirade. He looks sideways at a shattered Seema. He leaves the room, still looking angry, however, leaving behind three shattered women. Neeta walks over to the dressing table, tosses the envelope full of photographs into a drawer and shuts it.

(Flashback begins.)

Cut to Sasank, sitting in an armchair on the balcony. He rises and leans against the balcony pillar, lost in his own thoughts. Sasank then turns abruptly and enters his bedroom.

Cut to the interior of the bedroom. Sasank is sitting at the dressing table, looking through the drawers. He looks backwards.

Cut to Amu's room. Amu is lying in bed dressed in a pair of jeans and a sweatshirt. Sasank enters the room; Amu immediately sits up on his bed. Sasank goes and sits at the desk in Amu's room.

SASANK: Amu . . . I was told that you needed some money . . . Your mother mentioned it. Wasn't it possible for you to tell me yourself . . . ? Am I a stranger or something . . . ? Why d'you need the money . . . ? To go into business, is it . . . ?

AMU: Yes, sir.

SASANK: How much d'you need? Never mind, I know . . . Wherever did you get this peculiar fancy from? Business! Something I'd neither imagined nor wanted for you. I'd thought you'd graduate, at least . . . ! I feel ashamed to show my face to people because of you!

AMU: Let it be.

SASANK (*surprised*): Why?

AMU: Thank you, but I don't want any.

Amu looks very angry. He storms out of the room. Sasank stares after him.

Cut to corridor. Amu walks past his mother towards the front door.

SUDHA: Amu, where're you off to?

AMU: I'm going out.

Amu walks out of the front door. Sudha anxiously rushes to the door.

SUDHA: Amu . . . Amu . . . when will you return?

Sudha closes the door slowly and turns.

Cut to Sasank, walking into his study and sitting at his desk, cheque book in hand, with a rather sarcastic expression on his face.

Sudha enters and stands in front of the desk. She looks extremely angry.

SASANK: Your darling son decided not to take the money.

SUDHA: You can hardly blame him, can you; not after the way you spoke to him.

SASANK: Why? What did I do? What did I say . . . ?

SUDHA: What did you say? Was there anything left to say?

SASANK: You mean to tell me that I'm not even allowed to say this much?

SUDHA: But did you have to say it in quite that manner? You couldn't have put it in any other way!!

Sasank writes out a cheque, tears it from the cheque book and pushes it towards Sudha.

SASANK: Take it. Give this to him. It's the entire sum.

Sudha nods her head vigorously in refusal, then sits down on a chair and rests her head against the back of the chair for a few seconds before looking at Sasank.

SUDHA: No, I can't do it . . . Give it to him yourself, if you want to. You're only worried about saving your face! But what about your son? Have you ever thought of him . . . ? Have you ever bothered to sit with him for a moment or two, or to ask him how he is? . . . If you weren't willing to do it yourself, you might have at least organized some private tuitions for him . . . But no, you didn't. It didn't even occur to you, did it? Tell me, have you ever, even once, thought about the people in this house? Have you ever thought about me . . . ? Did it ever occur to you that I could've had a career, instead of vegetating at home? No it didn't . . . it never did. All you ever do is pore over your books. And a fat lot of good that's done you . . . Just look at Arunbabu . . . how well-off he is! (*mid-close-up of a distressed Sasank*) And today, if Amu wants to be independent in his own way, you can hardly object. He only asked you for a loan, you know—just a loan. And you had to give him a real mouthful. Now just suppose that he goes to my brother . . . ?

Mid-shot of Sudha and Sasank at the desk. Sudha has her back to the camera. Sasank is behind his desk, sitting with his face covered with his hands. Sasank slowly raises his face; he looks very disturbed by Sudha's comments.

SASANK : Your brother? To Samar? Is Amu going to him? Did he say that?

SUDHA: No, he didn't. But what if he does?

SASANK: No . . . no. How is that possible?

A very perturbed Sasank gets up and stands next to the desk, facing the window.

SASANK: . . . That mustn't happen. How can Amu go to him? In any case, he hasn't said that he'd go, has he?

Sasank walks to the door screen left. He turns at the door and looks at Sudha.

SASANK: You must . . . you must stop him, please. It isn't right, his going there . . . not right at all.

Sasank stands at the curtained door to the balcony for a while, then steps on to the balcony and leans against the railing. He is deep in thought, until disturbed by the sound of a car.

Cut to a dark room. Sasank is seen in silhouette, standing at the window at the far end of the room.

Cut to close-up of Neeta's hand near the light switch. She hesitates for a few moments, then switches on the light.

Cut to Sasank. He turns around and looks in Neeta's direction.

SASANK: Oh, it's you.

Sasank slowly comes forward and sits at the desk. Neeta comes forward, walks up to the chair and puts her hand on her father's shoulder.

NEETA: It's very late. Aren't you going to bed?

SASANK: Yes, yes, I will.

Sasank draws away from Neeta and leans forward on the desk.

NEETA: Baba . . . ?

SASANK: Ummmm . . . ?

NEETA (*kneels beside Sasank*): A penny for your thoughts . . . ?

SASANK (*looking distressed*): D'you know, Neeta, the only thing that counts in our world is success. Dedication's got no value at all . . .

Neeta hugs her father and caresses his hand. The silence is interrupted by the loud sound of the doorbell.

(Flashback ends.)

The sound of a bell continues.

Cut to the foyer of a cinema. Alok is seen talking to Neeta, then paying for a cup of tea.

ALOK: How much is it?

WOMAN: Four rupees.

ALOK (*to Neeta*): Come on, hurry up . . .

NEETA (*going up to the woman at the counter with her cup*): Thank you . . .

Alok goes inside with Neeta.

Cut to interior of darkened cinema hall. Alok and Neeta are sitting together. The sound of the music from the film they are watching can be heard in the background.

NEETA: It's been a long time since we've been to the cinema.

Cut to Sasank's study. The camera slowly tracks along the length of the empty study. Sudha slowly comes into view. She is sitting on a couch and looking at the envelope with Aparna's name written on it. There is the sudden sound of the doorbell ringing. Sudha is confused for a moment, then rushes to the bedroom and hides the envelope inside the wardrobe. In the mean time, the bell rings again.

> SUDHA: Coming . . . ! I said, I'm coming . . . (*As it rings again*) Arati! You're early . . . (*as she gets to the door*).

(Flashback begins.)

Sudha opens the door. Sasank enters, shivering from the cold.

> SASANK: It's freezing outside. I'd thought that it wouldn't be so cold this year. Serve me right for being so stubborn . . .
> SUDHA: Look who's here . . .
> SASANK (*looks in the direction of the study*): Why, hello! When did you arrive?

Cut to Aparna sitting at the desk. Sasank enters the study and sits behind his desk.

> APARNA: Just a few minutes ago.
> SASANK: I'd gone to get my pension. It's a fine mess, y'know . . . one goes and signs each month and counts one's money, and wonders . . . suppose one has a stroke, or an accident—or one's hand gets paralysed . . .
> APARNA: Oh, come on!
> SASANK: When I told her this, she said, 'They'll come and deliver the money. Even if they have to take a thumb impression, they won't give it to anyone else.'

Sudha enters the room holding a plain shawl in her hands. She hands this to him and takes the ornate shawl away from him.

> APARNA (*smiling at Sudha*): Did you hear all that rubbish?

177

SUDHA: I heard. That's the way he is.

They all laugh. Sudha turns to leave the room. As she does, Sasank calls out and hands over a cheque.

SASANK: Wait a minute. You'd better take this cheque . . .

Sudha takes the cheque and leaves.

SASANK (*to Aparna*): I've just finished the Irfan Habib book. Very good indeed.

APARNA (*smilingly*): Didn't I tell you? I liked it very much.

SASANK: Hmmmm . . .

Aparna hands over a journal to Sasank.

APARNA: Here, you'd better read this.

SASANK: What is it?

APARNA: It arrived today. Haven't you received it?

SASANK: No, I haven't.

APARNA: It's a rejoinder to that article of yours . . . you'd said it'd generate a controversy. Well, it has!

SASANK (*his face becomes grim as he reads on*): Good grief . . . what, what is all this? What is this he's written . . . ?

APARNA: Yes, it does seem as if he's furious, doesn't it?

SASANK: You . . . you know this person?

APARNA: I know of him. He's not from Calcutta, though; I think he's from outside somewhere.

SASANK (*agitated*): I'm a plagiarist . . . I've plagiarized the idea! I've plagiarized . . . ! ! PLAGIARISM! ! !

Cut to Sudha at the clothes rack, listening to Sasank fume and rage.

SASANK: Plagiarism! . . . He says that I'm, I'm not capable of dealing with the subject . . . That I've dabbled with it . . . I've dabbled! I've dabbled in the subject! Dabbled!! And look, listen here. He says, 'The writer has not got the foggiest idea of what he is trying to say.'

APARNA: I've read it. Read it twice, as a matter of fact. It was wrong of him to write in this manner.

SASANK: Wrong . . . ? This . . . this . . . is this the way in which one writes? Is this any sort of rejoinder? RUBBISH . . .

APARNA: I think . . . you should've been more careful in your article.

SASANK: You're telling *me* this?

Sudha enters and puts a cup next to Aparna.

APARNA: Yes.

SASANK: You're suggesting that I was careless?

APARNA: No, no. I didn't mean that at all.

SASANK: Go on . . . go on. Say what you want.

APARNA: Perhaps you wrote the article in a hurry . . . ?

SASANK: What're you saying, Aparna? Was this something to hurry through? Have you any idea of all the sources I collected the references from? Let me show you. There's no plagiarism here . . .

Sasank gets up in a rage, walks to the bookshelves, and starts to examine some journals.

APARNA (*as she rises*): Sir, please . . . please . . . what are you doing? It's not as if . . . as if he's the last word on the subject.

Cut to Neeta, standing at the door, looking at him with some degree of consternation.

SASANK: But why should he write in this manner? Like an imbecile!

APARNA: Write a rejoinder; a proper rejoinder. If you need any extra material . . . ?

Sasank has all through been scanning various journals from the shelves, but has quite obviously been unable to find whatever it is he is looking for. He picks up an armful of journals and sits at his desk, rapidly looking through their contents. A distressed-looking Aparna joins him here.

SASANK: But where's my reference material? I'd collected them from somewhere here. It should be in the July issue. Because if not in this . . . no . . . but . . .

APARNA: Just let it be, please. Please . . . tell me what it is you're looking for. I'll do the searching. What is it you're searching for? Which issue is it?

SASANK: Which issue? I can't remember . . . but I got it from here . . . I want to show it to you.

APARNA: Oh, please . . . !

Cut to Sudha. She enters the room. Sasank is still in a rage; he is angrily turning the pages of various journals.

SUDHA: What are you doing? Please let her look.

SASANK: She's hardly going to find it, is she? They're my things and I can't find them . . . how the hell is she going to find them?

SUDHA: Oh, come away, Aparna, and let him do what he wants. (*As Aparna slowly comes to stand beside Sudha*) He's always doing this, anyway—misplacing his things and then turning the entire house upside down looking for them . . . (*To Sasank*) Perhaps you kept it elsewhere?

APARNA: Please, Sir . . .

SASANK: Just one moment. Let me look . . . (*To Sudha*) You haven't removed anything from here, have you?

SUDHA: Me . . . ? Why would I move anything? (*To Aparna*) See?

Cut to Neeta, who remains watching at the doorway. Sudha turns and points to one corner of the room. She walks across to the corner and picks up a bundle of journals, turns, only to hear Sasank's furious voice.

SUDHA: Look, there's a bundle of papers lying here. Perhaps they're here . . .

SASANK (*off-screen*): Don't you touch them, I tell you; don't touch them!

Sudha momentarily freezes in embarrassment and rage, then puts the bundle down.

Cut to Neeta, still standing at the doorway. She cautions her mother with a quick shake of her head.

NEETA: Ma . . .

Cut to Sasank, angrily walking round the desk. He sits down on his customary chair, still looking utterly furious.

SASANK: Yes . . . don't you touch anything of mine. Just leave them where they are; I don't care if this room turns into a rubbish dump. I don't want anyone to touch anything here . . . Sit down, Aparna . . . !

Sasank starts studying the journals once again, to the exclusion of everyone around him. Sudha looks at Aparna and then walks up to the desk.

SUDHA: Must you read them just now?

Sasank carries on looking through his books and journals, without bothering to answer. Nor does he bother to look at Sudha. Sudha turns to look at Aparna, and then leaves the room. After a while, when Sasank looks around, the room is quite empty.

SASANK: Aparna . . . ! !

(Flashback ends.)

Cut to a dark bedroom. Neeta and Seema are in bed. Neeta's face is dimly illuminated by the light from a bedside lamp. Seema is lying on her side; she seems asleep.

NEETA: Seema . . . ? You asleep . . . ? (*There is a long pause.*) D'you ever think of Baba?

Neeta becomes rather preoccupied.

SEEMA: Didi . . . hey, Didi . . . ?

NEETA: I heard you. What is it?

SEEMA: Nothing . . .

NEETA: Alok and I went to the cinema today.

Neeta sits up and continues to speak, whilst Seema remains lying down, listening to her sister.

SEEMA: Which film was it?

NEETA: Just a film . . . I don't know why I was so reminded of Baba whilst watching it. So many thoughts . . . so many incidents came to mind. . . I couldn't even watch the film . . . Did you ever feel . . . feel that Baba had become very frustrated? Did you ever get that impression? From the way he'd get upset every now and then, suddenly, for no apparent rhyme or reason . . . He wasn't angry with anyone but himself, just himself . . . For not having been able to achieve anything. Y'know, he wasn't interested in money, or even climbing up the social ladder, for that matter. All he wanted was to show people how brilliant he was . . . But he couldn't, could he? Shall I tell you something? I don't think Baba was all that brilliant. . . I suspect that we just decided for ourselves that he was . . . And Baba himself soon began to think that he wasn't like ordinary folk. But really, it was us, his family, who'd said to him, 'You're not like anyone else, you're different from the others, you're much more important.' And we never thought, never even once wanted to consider, that he was like anyone else . . . an ordinary person.

Seema rises to sit next to Neeta. She is quite clearly perturbed by the direction her sister's comments are taking. But Neeta is oblivious to her sister's state.

NEETA: Just an average person like anyone else. You remember how you once said, 'Isn't Baba arrogant?' Was it really arrogance, I wonder? Or was it just a way of hiding himself . . . of keeping himself safe . . .

By now, Neeta has become very distraught.

>NEETA: Oh God! Seema, why'm I saying all this? How can I say such things? How can I even think such things about Baba? Seema, how . . .

A visibly distraught Neeta hides her face in Seema's lap, who comforts her as she would a child.

(Flashback begins.)

Music starts.

Cut to a dark study. Sasank can be seen sitting at his desk, which is cluttered with books and papers scattered all over it. The desk is lit by the light of a table lamp. Sasank looks visibly tired and preoccupied. The camera zooms in slowly from a high angle shot into a mid-close-up of Sasank. He pushes his glasses up and wearily rubs his forehead.

(Flashback ends.)

Cut to a high angle shot of a woman descending the stairs to the Roys' front door. She rings the bell, the door is opened by Sudha, who smiles in welcome.

>SUDHA: Oh hello! Come in . . .

The woman turns and looks upstairs.

>WOMAN: Rama, shut the door, will you?

She enters the flat. The door shuts.

Cut to Sudha's bedroom. The two women enter.

>SUDHA: Please, sit down.

The two women sit side by side. The guest is a matronly-looking woman, neatly dressed, with vermilion in the parting of her hair.

WOMAN: I've been wanting to come for the last few days, but I just couldn't find the time. And of course, you're busy as well ...

SUDHA: No, I'm not particularly busy. The children're in a bit of a rush in the mornings, of course ...

WOMAN: I see.

SUDHA: But after that ...

WOMAN: Well, you're alone all the time, aren't you? At least I think you are. I've never noticed you going out much.

SUDHA: Going out? Where?

WOMAN: Don't the children take you out? Don't they even ask?

SUDHA: Oh, of course they ask. I don't go.

WOMAN: Just as well, I suppose. All you get are questions.

SUDHA: No, no. I'm not scared of questions any more.

WOMAN: Well, yes ... Oh, I was forgetting what I'd come to see you about. My husband's been saying for days now ... but perhaps you people don't believe in such things ... ?

SUDHA: Believe in what?

WOMAN: In gurus ... miracles ... you know ...

The conversation is interrupted by loud banging sounds from the kitchen. Sudha makes an exasperated face and rises.

SUDHA: Excuse me. I'll be back in a minute.

Sudha leaves the room screen right.

Cut to the kitchen. Arati is squatting on her haunches, cleaning dishes. Sudha appears at the door.

SUDHA: Arati, clean the drain properly, it's clogged.

ARATI: Yes, Ma.

SUDHA: And don't dump the rubbish here. Throw it outside.

Sudha leaves. Arati continues washing the dishes.

Cut to the bedroom as Sudha enters and sits at the far end of the bed.

SUDHA: She can't do a thing right. You've got to explain each and every thing.

WOMAN: Will you come somewhere with me? It's a place I know—

SUDHA: Where's that?

WOMAN: There's a Swamiji who's come to town, a Tantric. He's got the most amazing powers. He can answer any question, and he's quite infallible. He really is a man of extraordinary powers; people come from all over to see him. He's staying with some Sethani . . . it's in the papers. Didn't you notice?

SUDHA: No, I didn't.

WOMAN: You can visit him once, surely. Come on, he doesn't want anything, nor does he accept a gift . . . surely there's no harm in going? I can accompany you, if you like.

SUDHA: Oh . . . I wouldn't want you to take the trouble.

WOMAN: No, no, it's no bother at all. I'll also have a darshan at the same time . . . D'you think that you're the only one that's unhappy? That I'm not all torn up inside day after day?

The woman's face becomes gradually sadder and she almost breaks into tears. Sudha looks away until she composes herself and even braves a small smile.

WOMAN: . . . I think I'll go now. He's coming back early today.

The two women rise and leave through the door screen right.

Cut to a shot of the front door of the flat, from the landing outside. The door opens and Sudha and her visitor appear. The woman hands Sudha a folded piece of paper.

WOMAN: Here's that address; keep it. Let me know if you ever want to visit.

Sudha unfolds the piece of paper and examines it briefly. The visitor holds Sudha's hands.

WOMAN: You will tell me, won't you?

Cut abruptly to a close-up of a handbag falling on a bed. The camera zooms back to show Neeta sitting on the bed. Sudha is handing her a cup of tea.

> NEETA: No, there's no need for her to take you. I'll take you if you really want to go.
> SUDHA: Really? You'll come?

Sudha offers Neeta some biscuits in a plate. Neeta picks up one and dunks it in her tea. Sudha puts the plate of biscuits down.

> NEETA (*nods*): If I asked Alok, perhaps even he might come.
> SUDHA: Will he, d'you think?
> NEETA: Perhaps.
> SUDHA: Listen, don't say a word to Amu and Seema.

Neeta sits up straight on the bed, brings her face close to her mother's and holds her hands.

> NEETA: I'll tell you this much, though, Ma. It's pointless going there.
> SUDHA: But I've heard . . . I mean, lots of people come to see him . . . they've had their wishes granted . . .

Neeta fiddles with the bangles on her mother's arm, the bangles that are a sign of a married woman.

> NEETA: A lot of people go to see him! So you've got to see him as well, eh?
> SUDHA: I just want to learn what he might have to say. Where's the harm in that?
> NEETA: Very well, Ma. (*Smiles*) At least it'll mean you'll step out of the flat. We'll go—one of these days.

Neeta leans back on the bed and looks at her mother tenderly.

Cut, to a portico. An over-the-shoulder shot of a man walking across the drive towards the portico. This is quite obviously the residence of a very wealthy individual. The portico itself is huge. The house is surrounded by elegantly tended lawns on two sides. The nearest house is at a considerable distance. Alok, Neeta and Sudha walk on to the portico from screen right. The man seen previously welcomes them.

> SUHAIL: The Swamiji should be arriving any minute. Please go in and sit down.
>
> NEETA: Ma, you go in.
>
> SUDHA: But what about you two?
>
> NEETA: We'll be alright here.

Suhail turns to go indoors.

> ALOK: When exactly will the Swamiji get here?
>
> SUHAIL: He should be on his way. Why don't you sit inside?
>
> NEETA: We're fine, thanks. But perhaps you could get my mother a place.
>
> SUHAIL: Yes, certainly . . .

The young man takes Sudha inside.

Cut to inside the house. A hall crowded with people, most of them sitting on the floor. Some, however, have only been able to find room enough to stand. The young man starts negotiating his way through the people sitting on the floor, with Sudha following behind him.

> SUHAIL: Please, come this way . . . please . . . excuse me . . . please sit here . . .

Cut to Sudha's visitor, the woman who had given her the address. She has quite obviously noticed Sudha and the other two.

Cut to Neeta, who has also noticed the lady, and turns away quickly. She walks away from the portico rapidly, with Alok trailing after her.

> ALOK: What's wrong?
>
> NEETA: The neighbour!!
>
> ALOK: Which neighbour is this?

NEETA: The one who gave Ma this address. She's over there. Come on, let's sit here.

Cut to the hall. The neighbour rises partly. Mid-shot of Sudha sitting next to a worried-looking young woman holding a child in her lap.

SUDHA: When's the Swamiji expected to arrive?

ANU: I'm sorry, were you speaking to me?

SUDHA: Yes, I was.

ANU: I'm afraid I don't know. I've been waiting for quite a while myself.

SUDHA: I see. But why're you here?

ANU: Because of my child.

SUDHA: Why? What's wrong with the child?

ANU: The doctors don't seem to know.

Sudha touches the child.

SUDHA: Why, he's got a fever.

ANU: Yes. It's been many days now.

Cut to a montage of various faces from the crowd of people waiting in the hall. Suhail's voice can be heard off-screen.

SUHAIL (*off-screen*): We're so glad that all of you've come to meet the Swamiji ... As you know, his schedule's very tight these days ...

Cut to mid-long shot of Suhail speaking to various people in the crowd, in an unctous voice.

SUHAIL: Please just hold on a while. The Swamiji's resting. He should be coming down any moment ... Sir, how are you?

MAN: Fine, fine.

SUHAIL: Baba was wondering about you, so I said ... I was certain you'd come today ...

MAN: Is your father well?

SUHAIL: Yes, thank you. And you?

MAN: I'm okay, thanks.

2ND MAN: Excuse me, but may I have some water?

SUHAIL: Water? Yes, certainly . . . Noni, hey, Noni . . . please give everyone here some water, will you . . . Goodbye, Sir . . . hey, hey, you lot, help all these people find places, will you? What on earth're you doing? . . . Please, sit down, here . . .

Suhail leaves the room gradually, organizing the visitors all the while.

Cut to close-up of the neighbour, who is craning her neck to catch a glimpse of Neeta and Alok.

Cut to mid-shot of Alok and Neeta sitting on the steps towards one corner of the portico.

NEETA: My watch's on the blink. What time have you got?

ALOK: Half past four. I think it's going to take time.

NEETA (*turning to face Alok*): I'm sorry that I've dragged you here. But you know Alok, we've not been able to do much for Ma. I thought she might gain some reassurance if she came here . . .

ALOK: How're the rest of the family?

NEETA: Oh, we're all alright. Amu's business seems to've steadied a bit. Seema's going to college . . . she's working very hard for her exams. And I'm fine, really . . . I go to the office every day, to the cinema occasionally . . . We're all fine; it's just that . . .

ALOK: What?

NEETA: Just that we haven't been able to explain to Ma . . . She manages the household alright but her mind is not in it. I mean she still sincerely believes that Baba'll return some-day . . . Just imagine, what if he really did return . . . ?

Suhail comes out of the house from the background, descends down the steps behind Alok and Neeta, and walks across to where a car draws up. A rather well-dressed middle-aged couple get out of the car. The camera follows them as they go towards the house.

SUHAIL: Good morning; I'm still waiting for Mr Ray.

WOMAN: Sorry we're late.

MAN: Good morning.

SUHAIL: Come in, please. The Swamiji's still upstairs. You might as well meet him there; it's rather crowded down here . . . Mahesh, take them upstairs.

The couple go in. Suhail leaves. The camera follows him until it comes to focus on Alok and Neeta, where it stops. Suhail leaves the frame.

ALOK: Sounds as if they're VIPs.

NEETA: Which leads one to imagine that we non-VIPs aren't going to be able to meet the dear old Swamiji for quite some time yet.

ALOK (*laughs*): That's all very well, but what if some of our friends see us here . . . waiting to see some Swamiji . . .

Neeta is seen smiling at Alok.

Cut to inside the hall. The camera slowly tracks across the crowd, recording a sea of anxious faces. It finally comes to rest on Sudha and Anu.

ANU: I don't think we're going to catch a glimpse of him today, either.

SUDHA: You mean you've been here before?

ANU: Oh, yes. But I couldn't speak to him; it was very crowded.

SUDHA: I see . . .

Cut to close-up of the neighbour.

Cut to a mid-close-up of an elderly gentleman with grey hair and a flowing grey beard. He is shaking his head in what seems to be acute distress of some kind. He moans in an inarticulate manner and slowly collapses. A buzz of nervous excitement permeates the hall. Suhail forces his way to the spot.

SUHAIL: Just a minute . . . please, let me through . . . Who's accompanying this gentleman? Is there a doctor here? . . . Is this man alone? Isn't there anyone with him? Noni . . . Noni, get an ambulance, quick. Please relax everyone, everything's under control; there's nothing to be worried about. One moment, please . . . let me pass . . .

Suhail rushes off screen right. Neeta pushes her way through the throng. She drags her mother away, whilst the neighbour looks on in utter astonishment.

NEETA: Come on Ma, let's go.
SUDHA: Why? What's wrong? Where're you taking me . . . ?
NEIGHBOUR: Neeta . . . ? Neeta . . . !

The neighbour continues to stare after them, amidst the commotion.

Cut to the interior of a metro compartment. Alok, Sudha and Neeta in mid-shot, sitting side by side in silence. The train comes to a halt. An announcement can be heard. Alok rises.

ALOK: Right, I'm off, then.

Alok steps out of the compartment. The train prepares to leave, with Neeta and Sudha sitting side by side in silence for a while. Alok stands outside and waves as the train moves on. Sudha looks at Neeta for a few seconds.

SUDHA: Doesn't Alok say anything?
NEETA: About what?
SUDHA: About the two of you . . .
NEETA: What about the two of us . . . ?
SUDHA: Well, no, he can't, can he? He knows that we're lost without you, that we need you.
NEETA: Oh Ma, not you as well!

The train continues on its way. Neeta and Sudha sit in silence, isolated from one another.

Cut to interior of Sudha's bedroom. Sudha is sitting on the bed, leaning against the wall. Samar is sitting on a chair, drinking a cup of tea. Amu is standing in a corner, behind Samar. Neeta takes the cup from Samar.

> NEETA: I'll take it.
>
> SAMAR: Thank you.
>
> AMU: If I'd known earlier, I'd never have let him go.

Samar turns in his chair and looks at Amu rather witheringly.

> SAMAR: Yes, well, we've had quite enough of that. Now let it be.

Samar rises from his chair.

> SAMAR (*to Sudha*): Excuse me a minute. (*To Neeta*) Neeta, can I have a word? And with you as well, Amu.

The three of them leave the room.

Cut to Nisha, as she turns to talk to Sudha.

Cut to Sasank's study. Samar, Neeta and Amu enter the room. Samar goes straight to the bookshelves and starts examining the books carefully. He rubs off some dust with a finger tip. A book falls; Samar picks it up and bangs it a couple of times. A small cloud of dust is raised. Samar turns to look at Neeta and Amu.

> SAMAR: I do hope that these books don't get ruined; they're not being dusted, are they?
>
> AMU: Who's going to do it?

Neeta looks at Amu.

> SAMAR: Why don't you people donate these books?

Neeta looks quite stricken at the idea. Amu looks downwards.

> NEETA: Why?

SAMAR: Donate it to some library. It can become a collection, in your father's name.

NEETA: No Mamaji, they're fine where they are.

There is a long moment of silence.

SAMAR: Where's Seema?

NEETA: At college.

SAMAR: Come on, let's go to your room, Neeta.

The three of them leave the study. The camera follows them as they leave the room. They walk past the room where Sudha and Nisha are talking in low voices.

Cut to Neeta's bedroom. Samar and the others enter. Neeta goes and sits by the window. Samar pulls up a chair and sits next to her. Amu stands a good distance away from them, leaning against the chest of drawers. The camera remains focused mainly on Neeta, with Samar almost being back to camera. Neeta is watching Samar very intently.

SAMAR: I wanted to see you people alone, to ask whether you felt that your father would ever return?

AMU: I, at least, don't think so. I'd say that Baba isn't going to return.

SAMAR: And what about you, Neeta?

Neeta does not say anything.

SAMAR: The same question keeps going round and round in my head: why did the man leave home in this manner? Without any rhyme or reason, he just leaves his family behind—suddenly ... Who'd have imagined it ... ? Amu, did you enquire at the bank?

AMU: Yes, I saw them last week. The money's lying as it was.

SAMAR: Extraordinary! (*Smiles*) He's not become a sadhu, has he?

AMU (*off-screen*): No ... no. That's not possible.

193

SAMAR: You people aren't children any more, so I can tell you what's on my mind... It'd never have occurred to me ... I mean, I still can't believe it... but your aunt said one day, in the midst of a conversation ...

NEETA: Said what?

Cut to Amu, alert.

SAMAR: That, that student of your father's . . . what was her name?

NEETA: Aparnadi?

SAMAR: The one who rang late at night that day ...

NEETA: Yes, that's right. Aparnadi.

SAMAR: Did she ever visit, after that day?

NEETA: She did. Just the once.

SAMAR: Hmm ...

NEETA: She came to give us some photographs she'd taken, of Baba.

SAMAR: Ah! She's a photographer, is she?

NEETA: It's just a hobby, I think.

SAMAR: Hmm ... And she's never visited after that day?

AMU (off-screen): Neither has Uncle Arun!

SAMAR: Umm ... Well, d'you think ... I mean your father, did he ... oh, what's her name again ... ?

AMU (off-screen): Aparnadi?

SAMAR: Yes ... did he ... I mean, with that young woman ... I mean, did the two of them ... you know, were they ever, how should I put it ... I mean ...

(Flashback begins.)

Cut to Sasank's study. Sasank is sitting at his desk and Aparna is standing behind him, her hands on his shoulders. They are both laughing uproariously. Aparna walks around the desk, to come and sit near Sasank, who has held on to her right hand all the while.

The camera moves back diagonally and pans to the left, to show Sudha entering the room with a glass of water and medicine. Aparna carries on laughing loudly.

SASANK: Well, is that right? (*To Sudha*) Okay, now tell me. Just suppose I suddenly became twenty-five years younger. What d'you think'd happen?

APARNA (*laughingly*): What'd happen is that one'd have to keep one's distance from you. Isn't that right, Bhabhi?

Sudha laughs at the sally and hands Sasank the glass of water and some pills.

SUDHA: Here you are.

Sasank swallows the tablets with a mouthful of water, then puts the glass down.

SUDHA: Drink all the water.

Cut to Aparna looking at Sasank fondly.

Sasank drinks some more water from the glass and puts it down. Sudha picks up the glass of water, and starts walking out of the room.

APARNA (*off-screen*): Bhabhiji, how about a cup of tea?

Sudha stops and looks back at them.

Cut to a point-of-view shot, of Sasank and Aparna, sitting at the desk. They look very cheerful and animated.

SUDHA (*off-screen*): I've already put the kettle on.

APARNA: Ah, you're great.

(Flashback ends.)

Cut to the kitchen. It is lit somewhat dimly. Sudha is sitting on the floor, kneading dough in the traditional manner. She looks very sad and distant. Neeta slowly comes into the frame and stands at the doorway. Sudha turns to look as she approaches.

SUDHA: What is it, love?

NEETA: Why, nothing . . . (*As she looks sideways, cut to a sleeping Seema.*) Seema's asleep.

SUDHA: Let her sleep. She's been staying up all night, for the last few nights. She's been preparing for her exams, you know.

NEETA: Amu'll be late, most likely.

SUDHA: Yes, so he said.

NEETA: Y'know Ma . . .

SUDHA: Yes dear?

NEETA: She never came again, did she?

SUDHA: Who didn't?

NEETA: Aparnadi?

SUDHA (*looks up slightly*): No. She came just that once. Why . . . ?

NEETA: No. . . I mean, just like that . . . because she used to come . . . that's why.

Neeta rises and starts to leave the room once again, only to stand and stop at the doorway once again.

SUDHA: Neeta, why don't you sit?

Neeta comes into the kitchen and sits next to her mother. Mother and daughter sit in silence for a few moments.

SUDHA: Neeta, did you ever . . . I mean, did you ever feel that . . . that . . .

Sudha slowly becomes silent; a look of intense distress comes over her. Neeta looks at her mother in an increasingly perturbed manner.

NEETA: What . . . feel what, Ma? What were you trying to say? Ma, tell me what it was you wanted to say . . . Ma . . .

Sudha buries her face in her arms and starts sobbing softly. Neeta looks at her mother for a few moments, then stands up and leans against the door, looking absolutely shattered. After a few seconds have passed, Neeta gathers herself together and leaves. Sudha still has her face buried in her arms.

Cut to a mid-close-up of Neeta examining the envelope with Aparna's name written all over it. She slowly walks over to her mother; both of them are looking much more composed now. They are now in Sudha's bedroom.

NEETA: You kept it from me for so long!

SUDHA (*holding Neeta's hands*): Never tell Amu and Seema.

NEETA: No, I won't. But Ma . . .

Cut to close-up of Neeta's hand. She throws the envelope on top of the table and opens the drawer. The envelope containing the photographs can be seen inside the drawer.

Cut to a mid-shot of Neeta standing outside the door of a flat. The door opens and an elderly woman appears in the doorway.

NEETA: Good morning.

OLD LADY: Good morning.

NEETA: Does Aparna Choudhuri live here?

OLD LADY: She used to. But not any longer.

NEETA: Oh!

OLD LADY: It's been some time since she left Calcutta.

NEETA: Would you know where she's gone?

OLD LADY: I'm afraid I don't . . . She didn't say. She comes to Calcutta once in a while, during the holidays and so on. She does pop in occasionally.

NEETA: And . . . you?

OLD LADY: She was my paying guest. Did you want to see her?

NEETA: Yes I did. If she does drop in, will you let her know, please . . .

Cut to street. A minibus pelting along at full speed, belching clouds of fume.

Cut to Arun's room. Arun is speaking on the phone.

> ARUN: No, no . . . I can't tell you . . . I can look if you want . . . She said she'd got a good job . . . Yes, outside Calcutta, yes . . . Yes, she mentioned something like that . . . So I've heard . . . She's got married, yes . . . I'll drop in one of these days . . . Yes, certainly.

Arun puts the phone down.

Cut to Neeta in her boss's room. She has been on the phone as well. She puts the phone down with a frown and turns, as her boss enters.

> NEETA: I've just made a telephone call, Sir.
> BOSS: That's okay . . . By the way . . .

Cut to street. This is College Street. Seema comes out of the Calcutta University building, looking very excited and happy. She hails a passing taxi.

> SEEMA: Taxi!

Taxi stops outside Seema's house. Seema alights.

> SEEMA: Wait here, will you. I'll be back in a minute.

Cut to a high angle shot of the staircase. Seema runs up the stairs.

Cut to inside the flat. Neeta opens the door; Seema is standing outside, gasping for breath. She hugs Neeta as she steps in, laughing all the while.

> SEEMA: Oh Didi . . . (*Looks sideways*) Oh, oh, the phone . . .

Seema rushes off to the study. The phone is on the desk, which is looking clean and dusted. It is entirely devoid of any papers, journals and so on. Seema picks up the phone, clicking on the dial several times, then bangs the receiver down in exasperation.

SEEMA: Get rid of this wretched thing. I tried so often to . . .

Sudha appears at the doorway.

> SEEMA: Oh, Ma . . .
> SUDHA: What is it, dear?
> SEEMA: I've got a first class!
> NEETA AND SUDHA (*happily*): Oh . . . (*Sudha embraces her, Neeta kisses her.*)
> SEEMA: I'll be back in a jiffy.
> SUDHA: Now where're you off to?
> SEEMA: I'm just coming.
> SUDHA: Come back quickly, dear.
> SEEMA: In a minute.

Seema dashes out of the room. Sudha and Neeta look at one another in amused perplexity. Neeta closes the door.

> SUDHA: Where on earth could she've rushed off to?
> NEETA: Oh, Ma . . .

Cut to a high angle shot of the street outside, seen from the balcony. Seema can be seen getting into the cab. Neeta comes to the balcony and looks downwards, with a smile on her face. The sound of a car driving off can be heard in the background. The doorbell rings suddenly. Neeta turns to leave the balcony.

Cut to Neeta opening the front door. Aparna is standing outside, looking elegant and well dressed.

> APARNA: I was told you'd been looking for me.
> NEETA: Yes. Come in.

Aparna enters. Neeta closes the door and turns around.

> APARNA: I'm not living in Calcutta any longer. Was there something in particular that you . . . ?
> NEETA: Ma . . .

Sudha appears at the door, looking very serious.

Cut to an over-the-shoulder shot of Aparna approaching Sudha with a smile on her face.

APARNA: How are you, Bhabhi?
SUDHA: Come in.

Sudha turns and leaves the room. Aparna's smile slowly fades away as she follows Sudha.

Cut to Neeta, looking at them going inside.

Cut to Sudha's bedroom, as Aparna enters.

SUDHA (*off-screen*): Sit down.

Aparna sits on a chair. Sudha sits on the bed, at a distance from her. Neeta can be seen at the door. Aparna looks increasingly agitated at this behaviour. The two women are both facing the camera and not one another.

APARNA (*turning towards Sudha*): What is it? Why are you all so quiet? Bhabhi? Neeta?
SUDHA: I wanted to say something to you . . .

Aparna turns her head and sees Neeta standing at the door, looking very sad.

APARNA: What is it?

Neeta slowly withdraws from the door; the camera follows her into the dining room, where she sits down and pours a glass of water.

APARNA (*off-screen*): What is this? What is it?

Cut to Sudha's bedroom. mid-close-up of a very perplexed-looking Aparna, holding the envelope with her name scrawled all over it.

APARNA (*sounding shocked*): Why, this is Sir's handwriting!

Cut to a close-up of a grim-faced Sudha.

SUDHA (*off-screen*): I found it in one of his books.

Cut to the door, where Neeta has arrived silently.

Cut to Aparna, who is looking more and more puzzled.

APARNA: It's my name. But why in this way . . . ?

Aparna's expression gradually changes to one of anguish and humiliation as she looks at Sudha and Neeta. She is still holding the envelope, as a look of utter disbelief passes over her face. She rises from the chair.

APARNA: What are you thinking? You people . . . you really thought that I . . . that I . . . (*She sits down on the bed.*) But I never even . . . never even . . .

Cut to an anguished Sudha, standing at the table, then Neeta at the door.

Cut back to Aparna on the bed.

APARNA (*abruptly*): I'm leaving now.

Aparna abruptly puts the envelope down, and leaves the room. She is crying by now. Mother and daughter look stunned at this development.

Cut to a low angle shot of the stairs. A distraught Aparna is descending, wiping away her tears. She slowly leaves the frame, as Sudha and Neeta come out on the landing, staring after her. They still look quite puzzled.

Cut to Sasank's study. The desk is completely bare and spotlessly clean. Sudha, Neeta and Samar are sitting at the far end of the room.

SAMAR: Yes, yes, I understand your feelings. This room . . . these books . . .

NEETA: These books meant the world to Baba.

SAMAR: I know. I realize that. That is precisely why I'm saying that . . . I mean, will you be able to keep these books the way your father did? Will you take care of your father's books the way he did his father's?

Samar rises and moves out of frame.

SUDHA: But if . . . if all these, these books are gone, what'll we— I—have left?

SAMAR (*standing at the bookshelves*): How can I make you understand? Look at the way they're lying; look at the dust on them. Instead of having silverfish and white ants eat holes into them, donate them to his college library. They'll not only be taken care of, but some people will at least be able to make use of them . . . I've taken the liberty of speaking to the Principal. He's agreed to house them as a collection, under Sasank's name. Just think . . . It's a great honour . . .

Cut to Sasank's study. Various people are removing books from the shelves, writing down index numbers etc., whilst Amu and a woman are cataloguing.

WOMAN: 155E/95 *Indian History Congress.*
156E/96 *Indian History Congress.*
157E/97 *The Wonder That Was India.*
158—(*A book falls suddenly.*)
WOMAN: Careful there . . . 158E/98 *Inside Africa*
159E/99 *The Cultural Heritage of India.*

Cut to Seema, standing at the door.

Cut to the staircase. Samar can be seen coming up. He crosses a man going down the stairs with a bundle of books. The voice of the woman cataloguing books can be heard in the background.

WOMAN (*off-screen*): 160E/100 *Medieval India.*
161E/101 *Lands and People.*

Samar comes up to the doorway of the study. Seema is standing there. He stands next to Seema and looks at the proceedings with obvious approval.

SAMAR: Started, have you? Good, very good.

Samar enters the study. Seema looks at him once, then at the books being removed, turns and walks off quietly.

WOMAN (*off-screen*): 162E/102 *Lands and People.*

SAMAR (*standing at Amu's table*): You should've got a few more staff, though. This is going to take all day.

WOMAN (*off-screen*): *Economic History of Bengal.* No number.

He surveys the room once, then leaves the study. Neeta is now standing outside, looking very sad. Seema is further back, standing beside the bedroom door. Samar gently pats Neeta on the shoulder and moves towards the room.

SAMAR (*to Seema*): Is your mother in?

WOMAN (*off-screen*): 164E/104 *Inside India Today.*
164E/105 *The Ascent of Man.*

SEEMA: Yes.

Samar enters the bedroom.

Cut to the bedroom. Samar enters and slowly walks towards Sudha, who is standing near the wardrobe. The camera follows Samar as he walks towards Sudha. She turns towards Samar, but refuses to look at him. Instead, her eyes are fixed downwards.

SAMAR: Believe me, these books'll be taken care of in the library. That's why the librarian's here herself. And I've spoken to the Principal once again. If he ever returns . . .

As Sudha looks up at Samar, there is the sound of thunder.

Cut to a monsoon sky. Lightning is flashing against a cloud-darkened sky, silhouetting trees waving wildly in the storm. After each lightning flash, the screen fades to black. The screen lightens after one such fade to Sasank's study. It is dimly lit, with shadows everywhere. Seema, Neeta, Sudha and Amu are all in the study, each of them partly obscured by shadow. The sound of the monsoon storm raging outside can be heard in the background. The camera slowly pans from face to face, before coming to rest on Seema. It cuts to each person as he or she speaks.

SEEMA: It's raining heavily once again.

NEETA: Like that day . . . exactly like that day.

SUDHA: Yes, it's been a year now.

NEETA: And what haven't we said about Baba in that year.

AMU: I said . . . that Baba never thought about us, that he never did anything for us.

SEEMA: I said that Baba was so arrogant, so conceited.

NEETA: And I . . . I said—that Baba was an ordinary man, just an average person, really . . . perhaps . . . perhaps Baba had also started feeling the same way . . . thinking that he was just . . . perhaps that's why . . .

SUDHA: I never told you people this, but for nights, before he left, lying in bed . . . one night . . . he said to me (*as Neeta leans forward*) . . . he said that the tragedy was that man had only one life . . . he lives just once.

The sounds of a tropical storm outside as the camera slowly focuses on Neeta's face. Neeta gradually turns her profile to the camera. The camera zooms in gradually to a mid-close-up of Neeta and lingers on her for a few moments.

Cut to a mid-long shot of the four, sitting in the darkened room. They are all preoccupied with their own thoughts and look very isolated. The end credits start rolling on the shot, before it abruptly fades to black.